FAKE NEWS

This edition published in 2017
by Prion an imprint of the
Carlton Publishing Group
20 Mortimer Street
London W1T 3JW

Copyright © Carlton Books Ltd 2017

ISBN 978-1-85375-999-4

Printed in Great Britain

1 3 5 7 9 10 8 6 4 2

The publishers would like to thank the following sources for their kind permission to reproduce the pictures in this book.

Noun Project: /Abir Alward: 159, 160; /Adrien Coquet: 120; /Adrienne: 11, 12, 14, 15, 16, 17; /AFY Studio: 65; /Aleksandr Vector: 20, 70, 107; /Alena Artmova: 56; /Alex Muravev: 9, 60; /AlfredoCreates.com: 54; /Alice Noir: 37; /anbileru adaleru: 180; /Aneeque Ahmed: 146, 176; /ANTON icon: 59; /b farias: 95, 122; /Benjamin Bours: 69; /Bonnie Beach: 156; /bulle ouvrera: 161; /Cards Against Humanity: 174; /Carpe Diem: 46, 187; /Charlotte Vogel: 153; /Chiara Claus: 53; /Creative Mania: 27; /Dabid J. Pascual: 35; /Datacrafted: 4; /Deni Sazhin: 84; /Dennis de Villa: 117; /Didzis Gruznovs: 42, 45; /Diego Naive: 7; /Digital innovation: 108; /Elaine Madsen: 163; /Eliricon: 140; /Elizabeth: 139; /елизавета екимова: 165; /enrico chialastri: 190; /Eucalyp: 186; /Evgeni Moryakov: 111; /Evgeny Kozachenko: 178; /faisalovers: 13; /Felipe Alvarado: 77; /Gan Khoon Lay: 16, 33, 52, 55, 63, 67, 71, 72, 75, 85, 114, 129, 171, 184; /George Z/Arztgeo: 6; /giacomo palmara: 44; /Gregor Cresnar: 18, 109, 125, 170, 181, 183; /Guilherme Simoes: 148; /Hopkins: 132; /hunotika: 136; /Icon Fair: 144; /Iconathon: 177; /IconfactoryTeam: 8; /Isabel Martínez Isabel: 58; /Juan Pablo Bravo: 30; /kesaryvamshi: 99; /Krisada: 172; /lastspark: 61; /Laymik: 78; /Lero Keller: 89; /Lisa Krymova: 6; /Llisole: 151; /Lorie Shaull: 25, 31, 65, 82, 83, 91, 107, 192; /Lucas fhñe: 169; /Lucas Rod: 179; /Luis Prado: 29, 106; /Mello: 82; /Mooms: 101; /Nathan Newell Griffith: 62; /Nick Bluth: 1, 11, 12, 13, 14, 15, 17; /Nook Fulloption: 105; /Oksana Latysheva: 162; /Peter van Driel: 39; /ProSymbols: 73, 126; /Randomhero: 124; /Ralf Schmitzer: 143; /Re Jean Soo: 92; /Rémi Mercier: 137; /Rodrigo Vidinich: 79; /Roman Shiyakov: 64; /sai aditya: 13, 21, 27, 33, 56, 57, 60, 61, 66, 79, 81, 82, 83, 85, 106, 108, 135, 136, 137, 139, 140, 144, 169, 171, 179; /Simon Child: 41, 97; /Thengakola: 112; /Thomas Helbig: 133; /Tokka Elkholy: 81; /Tomas Knopp: 119; /Viktor Korobkov: 103; /Vladimir Belochkin: 57, 66, 154, 185; /Wilson Joseph: 51, 88; /XOXO: 50, /Yu Luck: 90

Every effort has been made to acknowledge correctly and contact the source and/or copyright holder of each picture and Carlton Books Limited apologises for any unintentional errors or omissions, which will be corrected in future editions of this book.

FAKE
NEWS
"FACTS ALWAYS TRUMP TRUTH"

**Baron John Barron-Miller-Barron
and Professor Nicolai Dixon-Milhouse**

PRION

CONTENTS

PREFACE
...BY VLADIMIR PUTIN
but not *that* Vladimir Putin

PREFACE

ELLO, WESTERN FOOLS! YES, IT IS I, VLADIMIR PUTIN.

Ha ha ha ha ha ha ha ha ha ha.

I am sorry. That was a burst of evil laughter. It doesn't work quite so well in print, does it?

Anyway, I am Vladimir Putin – but not the Vladimir Putin you're thinking of. I am much less good-looking than that handsome son of a mother. Plus, I am worse at judo and at bareback horse riding. And I have less hair.

So, if you were thinking I was that guy, stop it now – or else! You have been warned!

Nevertheless, I have been asked to write a preface to this tip-top book that will tell you all you need to know about Fake News. A book that I can – with my hand on my heart – tell you has definitely not been written by my friend, the great President Donald J Trump, under an unconvincing pseudonym.

Speaking of President Trump, I owe him a very great deal. Actually, that's not true. I owe him nothing whatsoever.

He, on the other tiny hand, owes me shed-loads.

In particular he owes me some bed sheets from a hotel he stayed at in Moscow a few years ago and which now smell super weird. In fact, let's not beat around the bush – those bed sheets appear to have been urinated on by a weeing person or weeing persons unknown.

Trump is an old guy, so these things can happen. But those were expensive sheets! And that hotel room really smells of wee now! So, he definitely owes me some compensation.

Now, I don't know exactly what went on in that hotel room...

Who am I'm kidding? Of course, I do! I have tapes, videos, DVDs, you name it ... I have enough footage to make a ten-part series on Netflix.

But all you need to know is that the stains on those sheets are a curiously similar orangey colour to the "hair" on President Trump's head. And that's all I'm saying on this matter. For now.

But, that is all by the by, because this book is, of course, nothing to do with my friend President Trump and he will definitely not be profiting from it financially because now he is president it is illegal for him to do such things. Instead, this is a book that will tell you all you need to know about Fake News.

We, here in the great land of Russia – not that I am Russian, because remember I am not the Putin you think I am – think Fake News is great news! When the Internet first appeared, it looked like all human knowledge would be made available to everyone. As it has turned out there is more opinion, stuff people have made up and total bollocks on the Internet than anything else. And we, in Russia, or not, have been proud to make a significant contribution to this. So now nobody knows what's true and what isn't. And that's the way we in Russia like it. Perhaps.

Do you think President Trump got himself elected through his charm, good looks, intelligence, popularity and aptitude for the greatest office in the American state? Or was it because "we" in Russia identified him to be so incompetent and crazy that he would act like a great wobbling orange and pink blancmange-based bomb, packed with confusion, and denotat into the middle of the increasingly fragile American political establishment?

Who can really say? The jury on President Trump is still out.

Dosvedanya, capitalist idiots!

Your old comrade,

Vladimir Putin (but not that one)
Ha ha ha ha ha ha ha ha ha ha ha ha ha ha!*

*(that is more evil laughter)

9

FAKE
NEWS
101

//

AN INTRODUCTION TO FAKE NEWS

BY THE AUTHORS (ONE OF WHOM IS DEFINITELY *NOT* DONALD TRUMP – IF ANYONE SAYS IT IS DONALD TRUMP, THAT'S FAKE NEWS)

 Baron John Barron-Miller-Barron

Hi everyone! My name is Baron John Barron-Miller-Barron and I wrote this great great book all on my own. P.S. I am definitely not Donald Trump.

 Professor Nicolai Dixon-Milhouse

Hello! I am even more definitely not Donald Trump. I am Professor Nicolai Dixon-Milhouse. I am an international expert on Fake News and I am the co-author of this book.

FAKE NEWS 101

 Baron John Barron-Miller-Barron Follow

Welcome to my book. Many people are saying this is such a great book, it's so terrific, it has such great words – the best words! I wrote it all myself!

 Professor Nicolai Dixon-Milhouse Follow

Yes, indeed. Welcome to our book about Fake News. Fake News is everywhere today. It's all over the Internet and social media in particular. It's a subject that has always fascinated me. That's why I collaborated with my co-author to write this book.

Baron John Barron-Miller-Barron

I have not collaborated on anything. People are saying this is such a great book it could only have been written by one guy – the world's greatest living author, President of the United States...

...(at the time of writing), all round great guy and magnificent lover Donald J. Trump. I can neither confirm nor deny those rumors. To be honest, I should be able to confirm those rumors because I am the author of this fantastic great, great book... It really is so great.

FAKE NEWS 101

 Professor Nicolai Dixon-Milhouse

Yes, I should explain. I have devoted my entire life to studying Fake News. This has not always been easy. Many of the establishments where I paid to study Fake News turned out not to be proper...

...universities and were just scamming me out of my cash. Luckily, I eventually found a highly reputable place of learning and spent many years examining the history of Fake News, the ways in which Fake News works and the use of Fake...

...News throughout the world today. I have now put my many years of work and study into this book that I have written with my co-author – who is definitely *not* Donald Trump.

 Baron John Barron-Miller-Barron ● Follow

What is this guy talking about? None of us can be really sure whether I am Donald Trump or not. Not even me. Maybe I am. Maybe I'm not.

Professor Nicolai Dixon-Milhouse

Do not listen to him! Obviously my co-author isn't really Donald Trump. He's a narcissistic buffoon who comes out with a constant string of lies and Fake News. He is a very deluded individual...

...who sometimes seems to labour under the misguided belief that he might be the President of the USA. Actually, now you come to mention it, he does sound quite a bit like Donald Trump doesn't he?

Baron John Barron-Miller-Barron

Did I mention I wrote this book all on my own with no help from anyone?

 Professor Nicolai Dixon-Milhouse   ● Follow

It was because I am so fascinated by Fake News that I chose as my co-author on this book a man who seems to have no idea of what's true and...

...what's false. In short, he is a complete idiot who lies whenever he opens his mouth. I believe he is a perfect test case in my study of Fake News and falsehood.

FAKE NEWS 101

 Baron John Barron-Miller-Barron

So, welcome to this great book that I have written all on my own about Fake News – probably the greatest, most important, most terrific book with the highest ratings ever written. It really is so great.

 Professor Nicolai Dixon-Milhouse

Yes, welcome to the book we have written together about the world of Fake News and what it can do for you!

How to know who has written each chapter:

 Baron John Barron-Miller-Barron (definitely not Donald J. Trump)

 Professor Nicolai Dixon-Milhouse (diploma in Advanced Fake News Studies from Trump University)

THE BENEFITS OF FAKE NEWS

- Fake News is a fantastic new philosophy of life

- It is a technique for dealing with all of life's problems

- It will help you make a great success of your life

- It will make you wealthier, better looking, more intelligent and more attractive to others

- It will make you an all-round, greater, super, terrific, amazing person

- If anyone says that it won't do those things, tell them that's Fake News!

- You see! It's working for you already!

- There are no downsides to Fake News

- Fake News is Good News!

///

REASONS TO USE
FAKE NEWS

- Because you can

- Because it's endless fun

- Because it's a creative medium

- Because who's to say what's fake and what's not? – you may as well just make stuff up!

- Because it saves time researching facts and stuff

- Because it confuses and distracts people which gives you the chance to commit multiple criminal offences while they are arguing whether what you said was fake or not

- Because it helps identify people who support you – or, as they are otherwise known, gullible people

- Because it helps form a bond between you and your supporters

- Because people in general do actually believe anything you tell them

FAKE NEWS IS GOOD. BUT HOW GOOD?

FAKE NEWS 101

IT MIGHT STUN YOU, BUT I HAVE MIXED VIEWS ABOUT FAKE NEWS.

On the one hand, Fake News is really bad! The Fake News that the Mainstream Media constantly put out against great men like President Donald Trump is absolutely disgusting! It is a terrible slur on a man who is the greatest President in American history as well as being the most magnificent lover womankind has ever been fortunate enough to experience! It is nothing but filthy lies!

But there is another side to Fake News. I also think Fake News is absolutely terrific!

I use it all the time. It's fantastic. It's fun. It's creative. People love reading it. It helps you build up a *yu-uge* audience on social media. It gets everyone talking – which is a wonderful way of bringing people together in these troubled times – even if they are just yelling abuse and trolling each other.

And that's not all!

Fake News saves so much time on boring things like researching everything properly. And it is truly democratic – thanks to Fake News nobody knows a single thing. Most importantly you can use it to get one over on your enemies like that well-known illegal Kenyan immigrant President Barack Obama.

So, I think Fake News is an appalling thing and I condemn it utterly.

But at the same time, I think it is fabulous and I recommend it completely and I use it all the time.

Also, as far as I understand, which is very, very far, making up Fake News is one of the conditions you have to agree to if you want to win at Twitter.

 Donald Trump ● Follow

The mainstream media and Trump enemies want me to stop using social media. Only way for me to get the truth out!

THE BASIC RULES OF FAKE NEWS

THERE ARE TWO TYPES OF FAKE NEWS:

1. Fake News you make yourself.

2. Fake News that is stuff that other people say and which you don't like. Let's look closer at these.

The Fake News you have made up about yourself is obviously Fake News. Why?

Because you just made it up yourself, you numbskull!

You should never ever refer to this type of Fake News as Fake News! This will be an immediate giveaway! It will seriously undermine your credibility if you tell people something and then add, "Oh, by the way – that thing I just told you – that was Fake News!"

DO NOT DO THIS!

Fake News said by others is obviously Fake News. Why?

Because it's stuff you don't like and which makes you look bad. You should always refer to this as Fake News!

There are therefore two essential basic rules of Fake News.

1. Make up lots of stuff to make yourself look good and make people you don't like look bad.

2. If anyone contradicts you or says anything that makes you look bad, just keep yelling "That's Fake News!" in their face until they stop.

Armed with these techniques of Fake News you can achieve anything! And even if you don't, just tell people you that achieved it anyway and yell "Fake News!" at anyone who said you didn't!

EXAMPLES
OF WHAT THE MAINSTREAM MEDIA NEWS CALL FAKE NEWS

AND, THEREFORE, DEFINITELY ISN'T FAKE NEWS

FAKE NEWS 101

- Stuff which I (not Trump, remember) made up and which isn't true

- Stuff I was sure I hadn't made up but which still turns out not to be true

- Stuff which was true but which I got completely wrong when I tried to tell people about it

- Stuff I thought I'd seen somewhere but which it turns out I had made up and isn't true

- Stuff I would really like to be true but which turns out not to be

- Stuff about my political opponents which I am absolutely certain sounds like the kind of things they'd do, but for which no evidence can be found

- Stuff about great things I have done but which no one else seems to be able remember me doing

FAKE NEWS 101

- Stuff that sounded right to me but for which definite evidence to the contrary turns out to exist

- Stuff I read somewhere or saw on TV the details of which I have now largely forgotten or didn't take in correctly at the time

- Stuff I read somewhere or heard someone say on TV but which turns out to have been garbage in the first place

- Stuff I read somewhere or saw on TV which turns out not to have been a factual news report but some work of fictional entertainment

- Dreams I have had – even the really good ones

- Hallucinations I have had

- Messages from the spirit world that I have received

- All the rest of the stuff I say

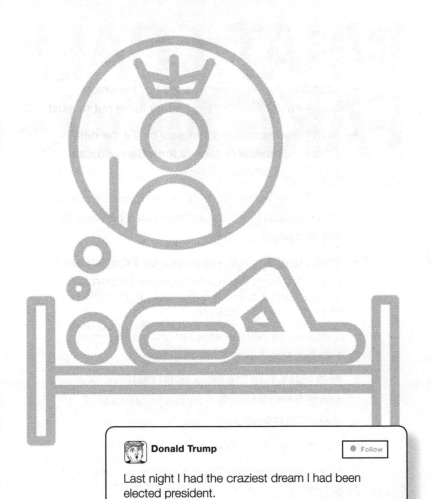

Donald Trump   ● Follow

Last night I had the craziest dream I had been elected president.

WHAT I CALL FAKE NEWS

AND YOU SHOULD TOO!

- Stuff I don't agree with

- Stuff said by people I don't agree with

- Stuff I might ordinarily agree with when said by people I don't agree with

- Stuff said by people who I might have agreed with but who I didn't like the look of

- Stuff said by me a while ago so I can't remember saying it and which is now contrary to stuff I've said more recently

- Stuff said by people I don't respect

- Stuff said by people I'm not getting any money out of

- Stuff that contradicts the stuff I've said

FAKE NEWS 101

- Stuff I don't like to hear

- Stuff I don't like to read

- Stuff I don't like to see

- Stuff that is a bit too complicated to take in so I can't be bothered with it

- Stuff I don't have to time to take in

- Stuff I wasn't really listening to but which didn't sound quite right

- Stuff detailing mistakes I have supposedly made

- Any criticism about me by anyone

DO YOU THINK PRESIDENT TRUMP IS GREAT — HE REALLY IS SO GREAT?

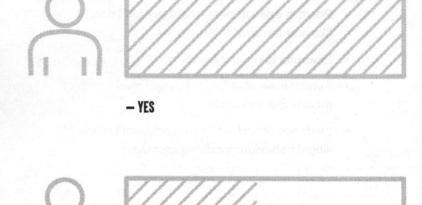

— YES

— I AM AN ILLEGAL VOTER AND SHOULD BE

DEPORTED IMMEDIATELY

- Negative opinion polls about me and the stuff I've done. (Remember, I'm not Donald J Trump)

- Positive opinion polls about people I don't like and the stuff they've done

- Lawsuits taken out against me

- Accusations of illegal behaviour made against me without evidence

- Evidence produced to support accusations of illegal behaviour made against me

GREAT THINGS YOU CAN USE FAKE NEWS TO DO

- Dish dirt on people you don't like

- Dish dirt on people you do like – but what the hell!

- Tell people about great things you have done – even if you haven't really done them

- Deny all the bad stuff that you know was definitely your fault

- Blame people you don't like for all the bad stuff that you know was really your fault

- Blame people you do like for bad stuff that was really your fault – what the hell! It worked the other time!

- Claim that it only looks like you did all the bad stuff you did because people you don't like tried to pin it on you

- Claim you have never met people you know extremely well and have been on holiday with

Donald Trump ● Follow

Did you think I would leave you cry-y-ing when there's room on my horse for two...

FAKE
HISTORY

"HISTORY IS A SET OF LIES AGREED UPON."

– Napoleon Bonaparte
(or was it, in fact, author Bernard le Boyer,
who was credited with the phrase In 1758?)

THE FATHER OF FAKE NEWS

THE GREEK AUTHOR HERODOTUS LIVED NEARLY 2,500 YEARS AGO AROUND. He is regarded as the first historian. But his account of the Persian and Peloponnesian Wars is believed to depict the Greek army in rather flattering terms. Herodotus is therefore not only known as the Father of History but also as the Father of Lies!

NEWSUS FAKUS – THE WORLD OF FAKE NEWS IN ANCIENT HISTORY

FAKE HISTORY

ANCIENT HISTORY IS LIKE NORMAL HISTORY BUT EVEN OLDER AND DUSTIER.

It is clear to us today that the people in Ancient History knew very little. For a start, all they knew about was Ancient History. And, even worse, they didn't realize it was ancient at the time and instead very stupidly mistook it for current events.

Little is therefore known about the people in Ancient History. But they only have themselves to blame for this. They completely failed to invent cameras or recording equipment so we would be able to see what they had been getting up to.

Even when they wrote stuff down they insisted on doing it in languages that no one speaks today. And if that wasn't enough, they would then break what they had written up into little pieces and leave it lying around covered in dirt so we have a right job trying to decipher it all today.

Essentially, the people in Ancient History didn't know a thing. And the things they particularly didn't know about was proper history – because none of it had happened yet.

They also didn't know any science and had to resort to inventing it all bit by bit.

On the plus side, the total ignorance of everybody alive during Ancient History meant that it was a golden age for Fake News! It was, in fact, an age when there was little or no difference between real news and Fake News. You could tell anyone anything and they would believe you! Only today with the benefit of the Internet, social media and, alleged, Russian email hackings are we beginning to get back to this happy position.

So, what are the lessons can we learn from ancient times concerning Fake News?

TROJAN
HORSIN' AROUND

THE TROJAN HORSE IS ONE OF THE GREAT USES OF FAKE NEWS IN MILITARY STRATEGY. It is, however, very rarely copied in campaigns today. This is possibly because modern armies are inherently suspicious whenever an opposing force leaves a massive wooden animal parked outside their military compound.

The original Trojan Horse story dates from around 3,000 years ago when, as we have established, people were considerably more gullible and susceptible to Fake News.

At the end of the Trojan War, the residents of the city of Troy woke up one morning to find that their long-time enemy, the Greek army, had suddenly given up and gone home. This was quite a surprise as the Greeks had been besieging Troy for the past 10 years.

Even more surprisingly, the Greeks had left an 80-foot-tall wooden horse just outside the gates of Troy as some sort of weird going away present. It was a gift to say, "thanks for having us during the 10-year siege of your city".

The Trojans stupidly thought this to be quite normal behaviour and regarded the horse as a lovely present since it represented the emblem of their city. They should perhaps have been alerted by the sounds of men in heavy armour shuffling about inside the horse. There must also have been a steady stream of wee pouring out of the horse as indoor toilet facilities had not been invented yet and 30 burly Greek warriors had just spent the night cooped up inside it.

Some Trojans suggested burning the horse which would have made the Greeks look much less clever. The Trojan king Priam, however, insisted that the horse was pulled inside the city as a symbol of their victory.

And then, while the Trojans were partying all night long in celebration, a battalion of Greek soldiers popped out of the back end of the timber equine like a series of armoured horse plops shouting, "Surprise!"

Great hilarity ensued – closely followed by appalling bloodshed.

THE ORIGINAL KADESH-IANS

OVER 3,000 YEARS AGO IN THE DAYS OF ANCIENT EGYPT, Pharaoh Rameses II aka Rameses the Great left a series of hieroglyphic inscriptions detailing his stunning victory over the Hittites at the Battle of Kadesh.

However, Kadesh does not seem to have been quite such a great victory for the Egyptians as the Egyptians had been keen to portray it. Perhaps most notably in his alleged great victory at Kadesh, Rameses had failed to take the city of Kadesh.

We know this because the battle was concluded with what is history's oldest surviving peace treaty signed in 1258 BC. Ramesses, agreed in the treaty, never to attack the Hittites to take possession of any of their lands while the Hittite king agreed never to attack the country of Egypt. The treaty makes it clear that rather than being a glorious Egyptian victory, the battle had ended in a draw. They didn't even bother with a penalty shoot-out.

Rameses' authorized account had instead described him charging the Hittites singlehanded, successfully riding completely around them and returning to camp unscathed. These accounts of the battle do not seem to be an entirely accurate record of events but rather a massive work of flattery for Rameses whom historians have described as "a stupid and culpably inefficient general.... (who) failed to gain his objectives at Kadesh".

There is only one possible conclusion – the Egyptian account of the Battle of Kadesh is Fake Hieroglyphs!

CROSSING THE RUBI-CON MERCHANT

FAKE HISTORY

///

FAKE NEWS WAS, OF COURSE, RIFE IN ANCIENT ROME. Ask anyone to name the most famous Emperor of Rome and some of the more ignorant will surely say "Julius Caesar". So that's at least one bit of Fake News he got away with.

While he was never emperor, Julius Caesar was a politician, military leader and one of Ancient Rome's leading authors. What better combination of skills could anyone have to be able to churn out Fake News to their own advantage?

After emerging victorious from Civil War, Caesar was instead crowned *Dictator Perpetuo* in 45 BC. This may have sounded even better than being made Emperor. Unfortunately, the "Perpetuo" side of things turned out to have been a little over optimistic.

Only a year later Caesar achieved something that would be emulated by many subsequent famous leaders – he was assassinated in the unfortunate "Ides of March" incident.

A few years earlier Caesar's political ascent in Rome had been assisted by his military campaigns in far flung corners of the Empire.

Obviously, there was no 24-hour TV news reporting at the time. But luckily someone took the trouble to write up an 8-book account of Julius Caesar's fantastically successful Gallic wars. The author was of course Julius Caesar himself. History, it is said, is written by the victors. Julius Caesar did this in a quite literal sense.

He did, however, want to make sure that his account of proceedings seemed fair and objective. So, JC referred to himself in the third person throughout.

Caesar had developed a classic Fake News strategy: go off to war and then write a series of books telling everyone how great you did in the war. Perhaps the wars themselves hadn't been strictly necessary in the first place. Maybe Caesar and his soldiers could have got away with just spending a few weeks away from Rome kicking back, drinking vino and enjoying a little holiday before JC issued his exciting 8-book Fake News account of the campaign like an Ancient Roman Netflix mini-series.

Along the way Caesar depicted his Gallic foes as lazy, backwards and prone to violence. The inhabitants of Rome were, by contrast, civilized, sophisticated and advanced. Another classic Fake News strategy! The Romans were suitably flattered, non-

FAKE HISTORY

FAKE HISTORY

Romans were all barbarians and Julius Caesar presented himself as the man to Make Rome Great Again!

He even threw in a line that would be turned into a classic horror film 2,000 years later:

"The whole nation of the Gauls is greatly devoted to ritual observances... in public, as in private life they observe an ordinance of sacrifices of the same kind. Others use figures of immense size whose limbs, woven out of twigs, they fill with living men and set on fire, and the men perish in a sheet of flame."

Unfortunately, Caesar had an overwhelming problem of a sort that has plagued many Fake News merchants ever since – he had a massive comb over.

Julius Caesar was a bit of a slaphead. As Roman historian Suetonius noted this was the subject of many jokes from his political opponents. Caesar therefore struggled to comb his hair forwards in an attempt to cover his shiny Roman *domus*.

So, possibly all Julius Caesar's political machinations and use of Fake News was so he would achieve pre-eminence in Rome and be allowed to wear the laurel wreath on his bonce and help cover up his shiny bald spot.

ANTONY & CLEOPATRA, COMIN' AT YA

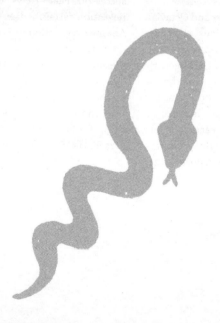

///

FOLLOWING JULIUS CAESAR'S ASSASSINATION IN 44 BC, a power struggle developed between his two closest associates – his general, Marc Antony, and his adopted 17-year-old son, Octavian (later the Emperor Augustus). The Roman senate had a bright idea to heal the trouble between the two. Marc Antony was pushed into marrying Octavian's sister, Octavia Minor. Unfortunately, this did not particularly help matters as Marc Antony was already passionately involved with the Egyptian queen Cleopatra.

And so, Marc Antony and Octavian embarked on a ferocious campaign of Fake News against one another. Octavian even invented the tweet. He was, of course, hampered in this by the fact that Twitter and the Internet didn't exist at the time. Instead, he issued coins which carried short slogans detailing Marc Antony's alleged failings. These reported that Marc Antony was a drunkard, a lustful debauchee and entirely under the control of Cleopatra.

Another possible piece of Fake News was a document produced by Octavian which he claimed was Marc Antony's official last will and testament. According to the will, Marc Antony intended to leave legacies to his children with Cleopatra including large chunks of Roman-held territory. The will also asserted Julius Caesar's son with Cleopatra (yes, she got around a bit) should be JC's legitimate successor. Fake News or not, this revelation certainly didn't serve Marc Antony's reputation in Rome.

In the end Marc Antony died as a result of yet another piece of Fake News. Following defeat at the Battle of Actium, he committed suicide when he heard a false rumour from Cleopatra stating that she had killed herself. **OOPS!**

REAL OR FAKE?

"IF I TELL A LIE IT'S ONLY BECAUSE I THINK
I'M TELLING THE TRUTH."

– Phil Gaglardi (Canadian politician)

///

REASONS FAKE NEWS IS BETTER THAN REAL NEWS

FAKE NEWS IS MUCH MORE EXCITING

Obviously Fake News is much more interesting than real news! Ask anyone!

The failing Mainstream Media insists on covering so-called "real news" which is based on "actual stuff" that's "really happened". How boring is that?

Fake News is much more thrilling. It involves conspiracies, record-breaking inauguration figures, people bugging microwave ovens and atrocities that may never have really happened.

Fake News is much better than real news. It's not confined by mundane real-life events. You can just make stuff up. It's more colourful. It's more exciting. It's more action-packed.

Some say it's fiction. *I* say it's like normal news – but with a vajazzle!

FAKE NEWS INVOLVES LESS RESEARCH

The Mainstream Media who make up real news spend a lot of time doing it.

This is totally inappropriate in today's world when people are short on time. And yet these reporters sometimes take as much as several hours to research, fact-check and write up their stories.

This is so inflexible and slow-moving. I leave these amateurs standing. I've made up ten incredible news stories and tweeted them before they've even got out of bed in the morning.

FAKE NEWS IS MORE PLENTIFUL

People are hungry for news. The Mainstream Media are hungry for news. They have all these newspapers and news programmes and whole stations devoted to the news. They need to fill up all this space each day with *news*.

Luckily, news stories simply pour out of me like diarrhoea out of someone who's recently had a past-its-sell-by-date curry.

I can fill up the entire news agenda. The Mainstream Media hate me for it.

But they keep reporting my stories and want me to appear on their programmes. So, I must be doing something right!

PEOPLE PREFER FAKE NEWS

I have many, many, many followers on Twitter. So many.

They all want to hear the news that comes direct from me. They don't want the so-called real actual news that goes through the Mainstream Media and becomes hideously distorted and spoilt by research and careful investigation.

These days, the news needs to be carefully crafted and manipulated. It needs to be sculpted and teased by professional craftsman into a beautiful and attractive thing.

The Mainstream Media refuse to do this. They like to just give people the plain truth of stuff that has actually happened. That shows you the level of contempt they have for the ordinary guy. The Mainstream Media cannot bring themselves to make up the sort of things that ordinary decent everyday bigots and other idiots want to hear.

Instead, people love to hear the news that I've recently made up. This then appears on the news and gets reported in all the newspapers and on all the TV news stations.

And that proves it – the things I say aren't fake. They must be proper news after all. Because they're on the news!

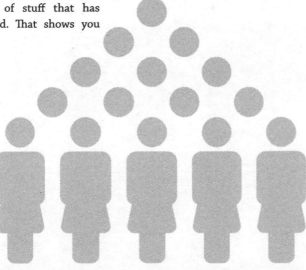

FAKE NEWS WILL MAKE YOU MORE POPULAR

Fake News will make you popular and gain you lots of new friends. I have been pumping out Fake News on social media for years now and I have gained millions of friendly followers in the process.

And as we all know online friends are real Fake News friends!

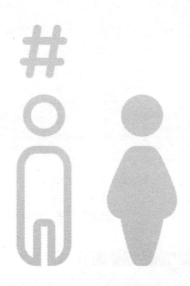

THE NEWS WILL BE JUST THE WAY YOU WANT IT TO BE

The problem with normal news is that it's often full of depressing stuff.

Even worse – if you are an incredibly popular and universally loved guy like myself, the Mainstream Media will find news stories that make you look bad.

This is *never* a problem with Fake News. With Fake News, the news is always exactly the way I want it to be.

And news stories about myself will always depict me as a terrific, *yu-ugely* successful and fantastically rich guy who has never been involved in any shady dealings or done anything wrong ever.

So, what's the problem with that? Fake News is Happy News! Well, it is for me and it can be for you too!

ANYONE CAN DO IT

Anyone can make up Fake News. That makes it much more democratic than the so-called proper real news which depends on actual stuff happening.

The elitist Mainstream Media don't like people taking their jobs, and pour scorn on anyone who dares to tread on their toes. They hate to see simple ordinary people making up news stories and complain that they're doing it wrong and haven't done enough research or waited for something to actually happen so they could report it.

But simple ordinary people, like my fellow multi-billionaire friends and me, don't have time to sit on our backsides doing nothing waiting for news to happen. Ordinary people need to stand up to the Mainstream Media and start making up their own Fake News. They need to open their mouths and let the Fake News come pouring out.

Of course, it helps if you are a multi-billionaire and have been voted into a position of extreme power.

If, however, you've got no money and have got dribble coming out of the side of your mouth, you're probably not going to get very far with your Fake News.

For me though it's not a problem. I literally make the news!

FAKE NEWS WILL LEAVE YOUR ENEMIES IN A STATE OF CONFUSION AND DISARRAY

This is one of the best things about Fake News.

When you come up with a really juicy bit of Fake News nonsense your enemies will be left frothing at the mouth. They will spend all day trying to work out what you were going on about and doing research to see if what you said was based on any sort of real stuff or information.

By the time they have worked out that it was another complete pile of horse manure something else will have happened to distract them. And if nothing else has come up to distract them, just come up with some more Fake News garbage to start the process all over again. Simple!

FAKE NEWS WILL GIVE YOU IMMENSE, LUSTROUS HAIR

Fake News will make you more attractive and make your hair appear like a vast and wonderful wave of monkey-piss coloured candyfloss sweeping over your forehead.

Even better, Fake News will ensure that no one thinks that this looks weird.

Donald Trump

● Follow

My hair is completely natural. I had it all transplanted from my own head and put back on at a slightly different angle.

FAKE NEWS WILL MAKE YOUR HANDS BIGGER

Another one of the many great benefits of Fake News is that it will give you bigger hands.

This only applies if your hands are unusually small – which President Trump's hands definitely are not. No! President Trump has big hands. No part of President Trump is small.

The only reason anyone could ever have possibly thought President Trump's hands were small could only be because someone once saw them holding another part of his anatomy (perhaps in a public convenience or while preparing to pass water over a hotel bed sheet). It can only have been the proximity to this other, absolutely *yu-uge* part of the President's anatomy that made his hands look small.

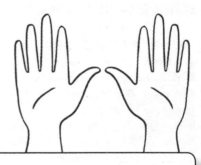

 Donald Trump   ● Follow

Look at those hands, are they small hands?...
If they're small, something else must be small.
I guarantee you there's no problem, I guarantee.

THINGS THAT ARE OBVIOUSLY FAKE

BUT WHICH EVERYONE AGREES ARE MUCH BETTER THAN THE REAL THING

AS WE HAVE ESTABLISHED, FAKE NEWS is more exciting and entertaining than real news. That's why everyone prefers it. This should be no surprise. It's a well-known fact that all fake things are in fact better than real things – as the following examples will prove!

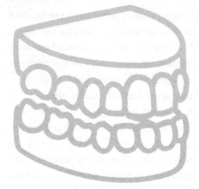

FALSE TEETH

False teeth are better than real teeth! Who has ever gone to a dentist with gleaming, shiny white, even teeth and asked the dentist to replace them with yellowing rotten, misshapen fangs sticking out in all directions? No one!

But plenty of people with disgusting teeth go to get their fangs fixed. And those who don't should be forced to against their will. I don't want to see any people with disgusting real teeth!

REAL OR FAKE?

ART

All of art is fake. Some of it is based on real stuff that the artist has seen and copied. Vincent van Gogh saw some sunflowers and did a picture of them. You can get a load of real sunflowers for just a few dollars. In Mr van Gogh's day they probably cost even less than that! But his fake copy of a bunch of sunflowers however is worth millions! Fake is clearly better!

THE SIX MILLION DOLLAR MAN

When I was a young guy I used to love watching Steve Austin play the Bionic Man on TV. He was a complete fake. He had fake legs and a fake arm and a fake eye. He may also have had a fake tan. But all these things made him much better than a real person. He could run faster, jump higher and lift heavier stuff. And yet for some reason the USA never entered him into the Olympics during all the time he was around. He was even worth more than a real person. The clue was in the title of the show – he was worth six million dollars! And he was played by Lee Majors. So, even the bit about him being Steve Austin turned out to be fake!

COSMETIC SURGERY

People can sometimes look quite ugly. Particularly all women past the age of 40. I know that's not a politically correct thing to say. But all reasonable women over the age of 40 will agree with me when I say they are past their use-by date and have nothing to look forward to over the final decades of their life other than the gradual disintegration of their bodies and being shunned by their husbands who are horror-stricken every time they look at them. Thank goodness for cosmetic surgery. Without it, I would tear my own eyes out rather than meet women 30 years or less my own age. Once again fake is better than real. Remember: do not take any of the above to suggest that I might be President Donald J Trump.

FAKE BOOBS

Now we're really talking! These are like real boobs but turned into works of art. They are created by doctors who are the surgical equivalents of Mr Michelangelo and Mr van Gogh but maybe not so much Mr Picasso. If Picasso did fake boobs, I don't think I'd want to see them. I should open an art gallery where the exhibits are not statues or paintings or any of that garbage. Just rooms and rooms full of fake boobs. Now that would be art!

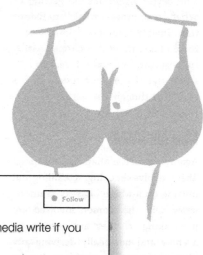

 Donald Trump • Follow

It doesn't really matter what the media write if you have some great fake boobs.

Donald Trump

I use only the best fake tan. It's called Don-seal and it does exactly what it says on the tin.

FAKE TAN

Who wants to see pale, unattractive people? I certainly don't. Slap them all over with fake tan to make them look a bit better. Again, it's like getting an artist to improve on reality. Except this time, it's someone in the back room of a tanning salon armed with a spray gun and a bucket of creosote. It's still better than having to look at the real thing though!

FAKE ORGASMS

Again – far better than the real thing. These involve shouting, screaming and putting on a whole big sexy dramatic show. OK, the women involved are just faking it. They are putting on a show and not really deriving any pleasure from the act of love. But on the plus side I don't care about that!

GOLDEN RULES OF FAKE NEWS

1. MAKE SURE THE FAKE NEWS YOU GIVE OUT IS DEFINITELY FAKE

Fake News is a great asset that you can employ to confuse and distract people.

But *do not* make the mistake of giving out a fact that is both well-known and demonstrably true beyond all doubt. Such facts might include: "The sky is blue" or "The Pope is Catholic".

Statements of this nature are unlikely to distract or confuse anyone apart from the very stupid, the very unobservant, the colour blind or those with little or no knowledge of the workings of major world religions.

If you are interested in making up some Fake News as a means to get one over on people, it is advisable to say things that are genuinely fake but which are likely to get people arguing.

Tell people, for example, that the sky is a hoax created by Obama, or that the Pope is secretly a Muslim lesbian.

And don't forget – do not make the mistake of then telling everyone, "Oh, by the way – that thing I just said – that was Fake News!"

2. WEAR A SUIT

Always dress smartly when relating Fake News to people. People are much more likely to believe any amount of nonsense you tell them if you are well dressed. A tailored suit is essentially the standard uniform worn by liars the world over.

Think about it ... used car dealers, professional conmen, career politicians. You name it. If someone wants to make a living by telling untruths to people, the first thing they buy themselves is a good suit.

As anyone who has ever visited a naturist resort will testify, most human beings are weird mis-shapen blobs with every part of their bodies somehow out of proportion with every other part.

A suit represents the best way that mankind has so far developed to shroud all the weird sticky-out bits and lumps and mounds of fat on people and to trick observers into thinking their bodies are attractive. A suit is Fake News in fabric form.

Once you have put a suit on, people will trust you. They will think you are a successful person who has a well-paid job and a normal-shaped body. They may think this even though the truth is that you are a completely unsuccessful and deformed person who just happens to own a suit.

However, this does not necessarily mean that they will then lose all suspicion that you may be lying to them. Once they see your suit, they may simply accept that you are going to lie incessantly to their face, and they will be happy with that.

Or, possibly, your shiny suit will just distract them. I've always found it easy to be distracted by shiny things.

3. GET REALLY WORKED UP ABOUT YOUR OWN FAKE NEWS

When announcing a piece of Fake News to the world make sure that your body language is appropriate to what you are saying. People will be less likely to believe your Fake News story if your body is telling them a different story to the words coming out of your mouth.

Say, for example, you want to tell people about some terrible atrocity such as the Bowling Green Massacre. This is something that sounds like it happened but which in reality you made up while eating an iced doughnut earlier that afternoon.

Even though you know what you are saying is untrue, try to look appropriately solemn. Do not tell people about this dreadful massacre while sniggering and grinning, or while looking weirdly excited, or while otherwise humorously gurning.

One particular expression you should avoid when relating Fake News is one of astonished or sarcastic bemusement. Others may react like this when they hear what you are saying but it will be very unhelpful if you join in with them. Do not stand there with your face telling the world "What the f***!" while your mouth carries on telling them your piece of Fake News.

4. AVOID GOING BACK OVER ANYTHING

Once you've come up with a terrific piece of Fake News you may find that people want to question you about it.

On no account let them do this!

They have no business to question you on anything, like your assertion that Barack Obama wiretapped you through your microwave oven. These people should just respect you, take what you say in good faith and go away and quietly digest the ex-president's sick and filthy behaviour.

Of course, it is tempting to go back over really juicy Fake News stories you have made up. But this will be like returning to the scene of a crime.

People will be desperate to hear about who, when and why evil President Obama committed kitchen equipment-based espionage. And so will you. You will start thinking, "Wow! That sounds like a great story. I want to hear more about how Obama bugged my De'Longhi E98C with Grill!"

Unfortunately, you might by now have forgotten that you yourself came up with the story five minutes earlier and will sit waiting in vain for others to chip in with further salacious details. Bad!

It's better instead to come up with a completely different Fake News story, which will confuse everyone even further. Or just pop out for a nice round of golf while everyone on Twitter works themselves into a soapy lather about whatever it was you said.

Never get drawn back in. It will cause you to doubt yourself and the great piece of Fake News.

5. MAKE WEIRD HAND GESTURES

While announcing a piece of particularly bizarre Fake News to people, I find it useful to make a series of weird hand gestures, for which I use my unusually *yu-uge* hands.

These range from randomly pointing at things, to throwing my *yu-uge* hands all over the place, to squeezing my finger and thumb together, to throwing my arms wide or just waving my *yu-uge* hands and arms around like a crazy person caught in the process of falling down a lift shaft.

It's like I'm having a fit every time I speak.

More importantly, crazy hand gestures provide distraction for those trying to listen. An impromptu bare-knuckle puppet show will grab the audience's attention and help prevent anyone concentrating too much on whether the things you're saying make any sort of sense.

Another plus for me is that waving my arms around and making crazy hand gestures will confuse deaf viewers who will be left desperately trying to work out what it all means in sign language.

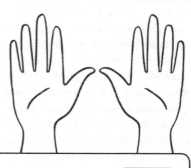

 Donald Trump   ● Follow

OK, everyone, let's have a big hand for the president!

6. NEVER APOLOGIZE FOR ANYTHING

One of my great rules in life is never to apologize for anything I've said.

There are three reasons for this.

Firstly, I can't remember much of what I've said. Not even stuff I've said quite recently. I'm a busy guy. By the time what I've said reaches people's ears, I have moved on to saying something else which also might not be true.

Secondly, I'm a smart guy. I don't make mistakes. So why should I apologize for anything? If someone tells me I've made a mistake, they must be wrong. They have either misunderstood what I have said or have wilfully chosen to put a hostile and negative interpretation on my words or have evidence to hand that I was lying through my teeth. Nevertheless, the problem is all theirs. They should apologize to me.

And, thirdly, apologizing is something people with less money do. Rich, powerful guys like me never have to apologize. The old adage is true – being a multi-billionaire with no conscience means never having to say you're sorry.

I never apologize. Why should I? So, if you're ever alone in a lift with me and it smells like someone's farted – I can tell you now it wasn't me.

A SUCCESSFUL
KOREA!

"THE SCENARIO ISN'T THE EXACT TRUTH,
BUT WE HAVE THE FACTS TO PROVE IT."

– Michael Curtiz (film director)

A SUCCESSFUL KOREA IN FAKE NEWS

NORTH KOREA IS A SMALL COUNTRY. SOME BELIEVE IT MAY BE EVEN SMALLER THAN KOREA AS A WHOLE. It is also very remote, cut off from the world, largely uninhabitable, has few natural resources and, for some reason, doesn't have a great reputation as a tourist destination either.

Nevertheless, North Korea, its current supreme leader, Kim Jong Un, and his late father, the previous and no less supreme leader Kim Jong Il, have proved an inspiration to us all because their country has become pre-eminent in one sphere: Fake News.

North Korea truly leads the world in the production of fabulous stories and information about its leaders which stand up too little or no analysis. And yet everyone who lives in North Korea believes it all! How wonderful.

What a brilliant example of just what you can achieve in Fake News – as long as you have complete and total control over the media and everyone is terrified of you.

THE INVENTION OF THE
HAMBURGER

AS EVERYONE KNOWS THE HAMBURGER WAS NOT INVENTED BY RONALD MCDONALD, Mr Wimpy or even the self-styled Burger King.

Instead this particular form of fast food was dreamt up by the former Dear Leader of North Korea, Kim Jong Il.

North Korean newspaper *Minju Choson* reported that the country's Beloved Father and Ever Victorious, Iron Willed Commander Kim Jong Il had himself invented a brand-new recipe. This tasty treat was given the catchy name of the "double bread with meat". Its recipe was a closely guarded secret although it is believed to involve a bit of meat between two bits of bread.

So, if anyone else ever tries to set up a business selling two bits of bread with a bit of meat in between them, they better watch out! They will owe a fortune in royalties to the North Korean leader.

THE WORLD'S GREATEST EVER OPERA COMPOSER

THE NORTH KOREANS ARE A HIGHLY CULTURED PEOPLE and if there is one bit of culture they particularly love its opera.

There are many great North Korean operas. One of the most popular is entitled 'Sea of Blood'. That definitely sounds more exciting than the 'Meistersingers of Nuremburg' or 'HMS Pinafore'.

The greatest composer of operas ever to have lived is not, as some might argue, Wolfgang Mozart, Richard Wagner or Stewart Copeland from the Police. No, it was of course North Korea's Unique Leader – Kim Jong Il.

Kim Jong turned out six operas in just two years, all of which are "better than any in the history of music." That is not the opinion of world opera experts but a much more objective assessment found in the official biography of Kim Jong Il and so it must be true.

Kim Jong's official biography also mentions that he wrote 1,500 books while he was a student. This means that if he was on a three-year course he was churning out more than one book a day. Presumably he was writing all the books he needed to read in order to study for his degree. And the word from North Korea is that every single one of them is completely unputdownable.

FAKE POOS –
THE WORLD'S MOST SUCCESSFUL PERSON AT NOT GOING TO THE TOILET

AS YOU MIGHT EXPECT KIM JONG IL'S official biography on the North Korean state website did not spend too much time discussing the Beloved and Respected Leader's toilet habits. There was no need.

According to the biography, Kim Jong Il never needed to poo at all.

Well, of course he didn't! He didn't have time! He was too busy writing operas and inventing hamburgers!

THE BEST PERSON AT MAKING RAIN ON DEMAND

THE DEAR LEADER KIM JONG IL also possessed an apparently magical ability to change the weather.

Theoretically, he could have used this skill to make made North Korea the ideal holiday destination with the perfect climate.

But for some reason very few people ever wanted to go there.

A DEDICATED BELOVED LEADER OF FASHION

AS WELL AS BEING THE WORLD'S GREATEST OPERA COMPOSER, novelist, fast food inventor and avoider of lavatories, Kim Jong Il was also a worldwide fashion icon.

North Korean Communist party newspaper *Rodong Sinmun*, announced that his zipped up overall-style tunic had taken the world by storm.

According to an unnamed French fashion expert, "Kim Jong-Il mode, which is now spreading expeditiously worldwide, is something unprecedented in the world's history."

So, not only did he invent the hamburger, he seems to have invented the zipped-up jacket as well. If you go out for a hamburger wearing an anorak, you owe it all to Kim Jong Il!

A SUCCESSFUL KOREA!

HOW TO SPOT
FAKE
NEWS

"NO MAN HAS A GOOD ENOUGH MEMORY
TO BE A SUCCESSFUL LIAR."

**– Abraham Lincoln (actually there is no evidence Lincoln
said this! So, this again is probably Fake News!)**

WHAT IS FAKE NEWS?

1. WHEN I DO IT

As I may have mentioned once or twice now, I am definitely not President Donald J Trump. OK?

Nevertheless, like that great, great man, people are always accusing me of Fake News. That is a lie. That is a slander. That is an evil calumny. That is, in itself, Fake News. After all, how do these people know if the things I say are Fake News? I certainly don't!

I just think of the stuff I say and I say it. Or I put it on Twitter where I have millions upon millions of followers. Probably more followers than anyone in the world ever.

It's my brain's job to come up with the stuff I say and my mouth's job to say it. Otherwise I don't get involved.

Or it might be the job of the fingers on my hands (which I have to tell you are unusually *yu-ge* hands) to type it onto Twitter and send it out into the world.

I am a busy man. I don't have time to tell my brain or my mouth or the fingers on my very big hands what to do. I just let them get on with it. That's

their job. And I let them get on with their job. I also don't have time to do much research about anything.

But I don't need to.

Do you know why? Because I am smart. *Yu-gely* smart.

That's why I trust the stuff that comes out of my brain and which my mouth and/or fingers (and/or any other parts of my body that may need to be involved) sends out into the world. If people want to do some research and check that all this great stuff that I made up is correct and accurate then I say, "Go ahead! Knock yourself out!"

However, if they do that research and then tell everyone the stuff I said was not right, that is the definition of Fake News! Those losers will have failed to do their job. And they will be sued accordingly. They should have done some more research until they found out I was right.

And, of course, the things I say *are* right.

Do you know why? Because I am smart. So smart.

People should give the stuff that comes out of me – out of my brain and out of my fingers and out of all the other parts of my body – more respect.

HOW TO SPOT FAKE NEWS

I give the stuff that comes out of my brain and my mouth and all my other bits enormous respect. I'm always very interested to see and hear all the stuff that comes out of me. It's all terrific stuff. The best stuff that comes out of anyone's brain and mouth and other bits.

And do you know why? Because I am so smart. I am so very smart.

So, I just like to think up all this stuff and get it out there to help the world. I am a mere vessel. I'm like some mystical guy who is receiving great wisdom from the ether and then producing more ether for others to enjoy.

Who's to say it's all Fake News. Certainly not these Mainstream Media guys with their fact-checking and research. What the hell do they know about anything? How dare these people say the stuff I say is Fake News! That's Fake News! It's the biggest political witch-hunt in history!

 Donald Trump   ● Follow

Sometimes I think I'm a wizard. Like the Wizard of Oz but with nothing to hide.

REASONS WHY FAKE NEWS IS NOT JUST THE SAME THING AS LYING TO PEOPLE

HOW TO SPOT FAKE NEWS

- Fake News sounds more modern

- Fake News is upgraded lying for today's interconnected world

- Fake News sounds much more official than lying – it's got the word "News" in the title!

- Fake News is also known as "Alternative Facts" – and that has the word "Facts" in the title!

- Nobody likes to be lied to – but everyone will find a piece of Fake News highly entertaining

- Fake News involves putting information into a coherent narrative*

- Fake News is something which you can accuse other folks of doing when they say anything you don't like

- Fake News is something you can do constantly to promote your own interests while accusing other folks of it

- Who's to say what's fake or not!

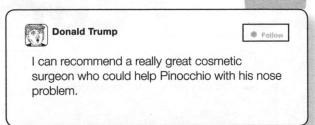

Donald Trump ● Follow

I can recommend a really great cosmetic surgeon who could help Pinocchio with his nose problem.

*OK when I say "information" I mean "lies".

WHAT IS FAKE NEWS?

WHEN OTHER FOLKS DO IT TO TRUMP

People are always coming up with Fake News about that great, great man – he really is so great – President Trump.

It is an absolute disgrace to tell lies about such an inspirational and completely innocent individual who exudes nothing but benevolence and love to all people.

 Donald Trump   ● Follow

HAHA! Obama in a microwave. Sad!

OK, maybe there's not so much benevolence and love towards former president Obama who – as Donald Trump revealed in March 2017 – wire-tapped Trump Tower via a microwave oven during the US election.

And, of course, there is no benevolence either for Crooked Hillary Clinton who, as we all know, almost brought western civilization to its knees when she downloaded some emails onto the wrong computer.

And then there's CNN, the failing *New York Times*, the BBC, the Mainstream Media, all liberals and

possibly for a load of other stuff we haven't thought of yet.

They say that the president has ties to Russia, that he has obstructed justice, he has attempted to blackmail, he is guilty of slander, he is guilty of money laundering, he has attempted to intimidate witnesses, he is guilty of conspiracy, collusion and fraud...

But so what if he did? It's not like he's committed any crimes, is it?

And even more ridiculously they claim that President Trump is unpopular. How can he be unpopular? He is the President of the USA!

Donald Trump   ● Follow

She looks so crooked!

women over the age of 40. He doesn't like any of them very much either.

But apart from that he loves everyone and it is absolutely disgusting and terrible that people come up with Fake News about the poor blameless president. Don't worry though. These people will be dealt with very severely and sued for all the dreadful things they have done. And

More people voted for him than all the other Presidents in history – put together! And more people came to his inauguration than that of any other president – especially Barack Obama.

OK, there are some photos that made it look like there were less people at President Trump's inauguration.

But there was a reason for that! It was Fake News!

The people who came to see Trump were all stood really close together because they were so desperate to see this great, great man more closely. So they all squeezed up into a really small space. The people who came to see Obama's inauguration on the other hand probably had to be bussed in – possibly at gunpoint, I haven't decided yet. And the people who came were all enormously fat. So *yu-uge*! That's why it looked like there were more people there. Obama only bussed in really obese people. And it is a well-known fact that those obese people take up more space.

So, that's what made it look like that more people turned out for Obama!

It was because Obama encourages poor health and obesity and all his supporters are disgusting and obese!

Donald Trump   ● Follow

A typical Obama supporter. That's what Obamacare does!

CLASSIC FAKE NEWS

"DON'T BELIEVE ANY FALSE RUMOURS UNLESS YOU HEAR THEM FROM ME."

– Vic Schiro (Mayor of New Orleans)

CLASSIC EXAMPLES OF FAKE NEWS 1

THE CROWD AT TRUMP'S INAUGURATION WAS THE BIGGEST IN HISTORY

Donald Trump spent his first day in office as US President in January 2017 summoning news reporters to tell them about the most important matter currently concerning the brand-new administration – the size of the crowd that had turned up for his inauguration the previous day.

Trump then went to the CIA's headquarters to address his loyal staff of intelligence officers. While standing in front of a wall honouring officers who had died in service he told the current staff all about the size of his inauguration crowd. "Looked like a million, a million and a half people," he told them and it had gone, "all the way back to the Washington Monument."

Later that day Trump sent out his then press secretary Sean Spicer for the administration's first press briefing. Spicer stepped out to address the world's press on the new administration's pressing and immediate concerns – the size of the crowd at the inauguration.

Spicer told the press that Trump had had, "the largest audience ever to witness an inauguration, period, both in person and around the globe." He went on to say that photos of the inauguration had been, "Intentionally framed in a way to minimize the enormous support that had gathered on the National Mall."

The photos of Trump's inauguration had clearly been "intentionally framed" by the anti-Trump media. We know this because the pictures made it clear very few came to see Trump.

The media had even gone so far as to "intentionally frame" pictures of Obama's inauguration by taking photos from exactly the same angle at exactly the same time of day to make it look like loads of people had turned out for his swearing in in 2009.

But obviously that couldn't be true?! The fact that it looked like there were twice as many people at Obama's inauguration compared to Trump's must have been an optical illusion.

And yet still some people chose to believe their own eyes rather than what the White House was telling them.

Could this mean that Sean Spicer's claims about the crowd size were falsehoods. No, they were "alternative facts" as Trump campaign strategist Kellyanne Conway explained in a TV interview the following day.

So, that is another a handy phrase to use when peddling Fake News!

Even if you are caught out by incontrovertible evidence or when everyone can see photos which clearly show thousands more people attended Obama's inauguration than yours – never admit that you were lying – just say you were using "alternative facts"!

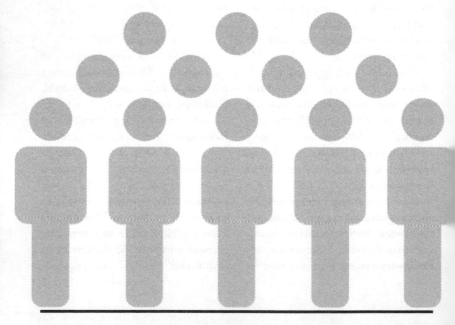

CLASSIC EXAMPLES OF FAKE NEWS 2

CLIMATE CHANGE IS A HOAX!

In November 2012, Donald Trump tweeted that "The concept of global warming was created by and for the Chinese in order to make U.S. manufacturing non-competitive". In December 2013, he complained about cold weather during the winter saying, "Global warming is a total, and very expensive, hoax!"

His tweets carried on into January 2014: "*NBC News* just called it the great freeze – coldest weather in years. Is our country still spending money on the GLOBAL WARMING HOAX?"

Good point! If global warming is true why does it still get a bit chilly in the middle of winter?

Clearly this overwhelming evidence against global warming has escaped the notice of the world's climate scientists. Presumably this is because these scientists are all being paid by the Chinese to promote what Trump called "this very expensive GLOBAL WARMING bullshit".

And indeed, Trump spotted a clever ploy that the climate scientists had suddenly decided to instigate to keep their Chinese paymasters happy:

On 29th January 2014, Trump tweeted: "The weather has been so cold for so long that the global warming HOAXSTERS were forced to change the name to Climate Change to keep $ flow!"

CLASSIC EXAMPLES OF FAKE NEWS 3

THE POPE BACKS TRUMP

In July 2016, during the presidential campaign, a story appeared on an American website saying that the Pope had endorsed Donald Trump in the forthcoming election.

Well, what's so odd about that!?

OK, the Pope had said the previous February that because of his threats to build a wall with Mexico and deport immigrants, Trump was not a Christian. So, in a sense the Pope had excommunicated Trump only to then sensationally change his mind and back him in the election. Perhaps the Pope had placed a significant bet on Trump winning. Who knows?

After all there were many similarities between the two men as Trump himself noted in his Christmas day tweet in December 2013:

"The new Pope is a humble man, very much like me, which probably explains why I like him so much!"

In May 2017, the two men met and the joy and excitement was clearly visible on the Pope's face in photos recording the event. The meeting filled Trump with great religious inspiration causing him to tweet: "I leave the Vatican more determined than ever to pursue PEACE in our world."

Unfortunately, Trump's sense of religious benevolence did not extend to his devoted press secretary Sean Spicer who was accompanying the President on this foreign trip. Spicer is a devout Catholic for whom meeting the pontiff would literally have been the greatest moment of his entire life.

Trump did not however fix it for Spicer to meet the Pope! Sad!

CLASSIC EXAMPLES OF FAKE NEWS 4

VOTER FRAUD COST TRUMP THE POPULAR VOTE IN THE PRESIDENTIAL ELECTION

Donald Trump won the 2016 election with 306 electoral college votes against Hillary Clinton's 232.

In terms of actual votes cast however Hillary Clinton won 65.9 million against 63 million for Trump.

So, more people voted for Hillary than for Trump.

If only it were possible to devise a system where the actual total number of votes was used to elect the president. If only it were possible to just count the total votes cast and say whoever got the most was president. This system would then show that more than 2.5 million more people wanted Clinton than Trump...

But no. Such a system is obviously completely impossible. Instead the votes have to be translated into a number of "electoral college" seats which are allocated to each state.

Still the fact that more people had voted for Clinton than Trump suggested something must be wrong! Could it be the distortions caused by the electoral college system? Trump himself had railed against its vagaries on November 6, 2012, when he tweeted:

"The electoral college is a disaster for a democracy."

However, when this procedure proved helpful to his own presidential bid, he changed his tune ever so slightly. On November 15, 2016, he tweeted:

"The Electoral College is actually genius in that it brings all states, including the smaller ones, into play."

But still the fact that more people had voted for Hillary Clinton than for himself rankled. And so, on November 27, 2016, Trump tweeted:

"In addition to winning the Electoral College in a landslide, I won the popular vote if you deduct the millions of people who voted illegally."

Ah ha! That was it! There was no distortion caused by the electoral college system! It simply was not possible that more people could have voted for Hillary Clinton than for Trump. Therefore, the only possible explanation was voter fraud.

OK, there didn't seem to be any evidence of this whatsoever. But that's just nit-picking!

CLASSIC EXAMPLES OF FAKE NEWS 5

OBAMA WIRETAPPED TRUMP TOWER IN THE RUN UP TO THE 2016 ELECTION

Beginning at 5.35 am eastern standard time on March 4, 2017, (yes, he was up at 5.35 in the morning to do this), Donald Trump began a run of tweets accusing former President Barack Obama of having wiretapped him during the 2016 election:

"Terrible! Just found out that Obama had my 'wires tapped' in Trump Tower just before the victory. Nothing found. This is McCarthyism!"

Trump continued:

"Is it legal for a sitting President to be "wiretapping" a race for president prior to an election? Turned down by court earlier. A NEW LOW!"

And then he carried on tweeting even more:

"How low has President Obama gone to tap my phones during the very sacred election process. This is Nixon/Watergate. Bad (or sick) guy!"

After this devastating exposure of extraordinary political abuse, Trump seemed to forget the subject completely and is believed to have popped out for a few rounds of golf.

Although no evidence to back up the claims seemed to be forthcoming, Trump strategist Kellyanne Conway announced on TV that, "There are many ways to surveil each other now, unfortunately," including, "microwaves that turn into cameras, etc."

So, that's how Obama did it! He bugged Trump's microwave oven presumably in an effort to find out exactly what ready meals the president elect was eating.

HOPELESS HOAXES

"YOU CAN FOOL SOME OF THE PEOPLE ALL OF THE TIME, AND ALL OF THE PEOPLE SOME OF THE TIME, BUT YOU CANNOT FOOL ALL OF THE PEOPLE ALL OF THE TIME."

– Abraham Lincoln

(again attributed to Lincoln, but no-one can prove he said it!)

HISTORIC HOAXES
THAT ENDED UP GOING
A BIT WRONG

A HOAX IS A BIG TRICK played on people based on what might seem a small and corny idea. Hence the well-known adage: "Mighty hoax from little cornies grow."

No! You're wrong! That was (according to Fake News) a fantastic and hilarious joke!

The world of hoaxes is however another great area in which the exponents of Fake News have plied their trade through the centuries – sometimes with rather unfortunate unintended consequences.

ORSON AROUND
– PROBABLY THE BEST HOAX
IN THE WORLD

ORSON WELLES' RADIO **PRODUCTION OF** *War of the Worlds* was literally Fake News. Broadcast on October 30, 1938, the programme related HG Wells' tale of a Martian invasion of Earth in the form of a hoax news report. The event has since become infamous for the panic it caused among its listeners. It may however be not the radio show but the stories of panic that were the hoax.

The programme was a scripted performance by the then 23-year-old Orson Welles and his Mercury Theatre company. Welles had had the idea of "doing a radio broadcast in such a manner that a crisis would actually seem to be happening ... a real event taking place at that time, rather than a mere radio play."

But guess what! This idea of using a radio broadcast to play a hoax on the listeners wasn't an original idea at all!

A number of earlier radio shows had used the same technique. The BBC had broadcast a hoax news report about a riot in London in 1926 and a year later in Adelaide, Australia station 5CL had aired a fake report of an air attack on the city's port.

Some listeners were taken in by the Australian broadcast but their response was not to descend into mass panic or take to the streets. Instead, they did what any ordinary, decent people would do: they jammed the radio station's phone switchboard to ask what the heck was going on.

When Americans tuned in to Orson Welles' *War of the Worlds* in

1938, they heard meteors landing in fields in New Jersey, Chicago and St Louis, monstrous Martians emerging from them and advancing across the USA and the annihilation of 7,000 National Guardsman by Martian death rays – all supposedly happening "live" on air!

The next morning, newspaper headlines across the nation detailed the panic and social breakdown that had resulted from the broadcast.

The *New York Times* headline read: "Radio Listeners in Panic Taking War Drama As Fact", the *Boston Globe* ran with: "Radio Play Terrifies Nation"; and the *Daily News* said "Fake Radio 'War' Stirs Terror Through US".

That other ever-reliable source of information Adolf Hitler chipped into the debate saying that the resulting panic provided "evidence of the decadence and corrupt condition of democracy."

So, were people treated for shock in New York's hospitals? Had anyone had a heart attack as a result of listening to the show?

No! It turned out to that the newspapers were the real hoaxers. As in the Australian broadcast 11 years earlier, a few people had phoned in to ask what was happening while a few

hundred others wrote to complain about it over the next few days. But that sort of thing wouldn't have made for dramatic newspaper headlines.

The real truth of the matter was that only 2 per cent of the US population listened to Welles' drama. And few – if any – took to the streets in panic.

Most people were listening to ventriloquist Edgar Bergen and his dummy Charlie McCarthy who were appearing on a different channel at the same time.

It is not recorded how many of these listeners took to the streets in terror because a little wooden man with a monocle had been brought to life on national radio.

FAKE ZOOS!

ANOTHER EXAMPLE OF THE POWER of Fake News had been seen in New York 64 years before Orson Welles' supposed *War of the Worlds* debacle.

In November 1874, New Yorkers had taken to the streets in terror as a result of another media hoax.

The panic followed the publication in the *New York Herald* of a lead story claiming that there had been a mass breakout from a secure facility in the heart of the city – Central Park Zoo.

The chilling headlines claimed an "Awful Calamity" had occurred with "Terrible Scenes of Mutilation."

Dreadful though the news was, it wasn't good enough to make the newspaper's front page. The *Herald*'s front page was instead covered with adverts. Readers had to rustle past these to page three to learn that the city in which they lived had just endured "A Shocking Sabbath Carnival of Death."

A rhinoceros had kebabed his keeper to death and broken free first before deciding to release some of his fellow zoological detainees.

The rhino was now in the New York sewers while a polar bear, a panther, some hyenas and a tiger were on the streets of Manhattan and a Numidian lion had been spotted in a church.

Forty-nine New Yorkers had been killed while hundreds more injured and the police and authorities were still battling to control the situation.

Upon learning of these horrors, the readers of the *New York Herald* all exclaimed as one: "Gordon Bennett!"

And indeed, the editor and owner of the *New York Herald*, Gordon Bennett (of "Gordon Bennett!" fame) was the man responsible for this horrifying but completely fictitious story.

In Bennett's defence, the piece about the zoo breakout concluded by telling readers: "Of course, the entire story given above is a pure

HOPELESS HOAXES

fabrication... Not a single act or incident described has taken place."

Unfortunately, many had not bothered to read that far because they were already panicking and rushing into the streets to defend their homes.

The *Herald* had been established by Bennett's father, James Gordon Bennett senior, who believed "the object of the modern newspaper is not to instruct, but to startle and amuse." Bennett junior went one step further than his dad. He believed a newspaper's job was not merely to report the news but to create it and to orchestrate dramatic events that would get people talking. Or, as in this case, shrieking in bloody terror.

This clearly demonstrates how Fake News can be a significant benefit to newspaper profits! You can just report the facts. Or you can fraudulently make stuff up to provoke terror and chaos then sell more newspapers reporting on all the terror and chaos!

CARSON AROUND FAKE LOOS!

WE HAVE ESTABLISHED THEN that one of the most important principles in Fake News is to get people terrified over something. And if there's one thing that would surely worry everyone it's a shortage of toilet paper. Everyone that is with the exception of Kim Jong Il because (as we have established) he never had to poo.

In late 1973, Harold V Froelich, a US Republican congressman for a heavily forested area of Wisconsin, became concerned about a reduced stream of paper pulp. In November, he released a press statement asking if the US government was facing "a serious shortage of paper".

No one seemed very bothered by this. And so, in December, Froelich tried again. On this occasion, he hit the big time when he issued a press release warning of an impending toilet paper shortage.

This loo roll famine would be "no laughing matter" warned Froelich but "a problem that will potentially touch every American."

And Americans knew exactly where a toilet paper shortage would touch them.

US talk show host Johnny Carson picked up on the story and joked about it on *The Tonight Show*.

"You know," said Carson, "we've got all sorts of shortages these days. But have you heard the latest? I'm not kidding. I saw it in the papers. There's a shortage of toilet paper!"

The next day panic buying of toilet

paper ensued. Shops quickly sold out of toilet paper. Even if there hadn't been a toilet paper crisis before, there was now!

People were getting very worried. In fact, they became so worried it probably made them desperate for even more toilet paper!

BOOM, BOOM!

ONLY ONE THING IS MORE TERRIFYING THAN A LACK OF TOILET PAPER AND THAT IS A BOMB THREAT.

And only one thing is more terrifying than a bomb threat – a bomb threat during a toilet paper shortage.

Sadly, people no longer seem to find bomb hoax warnings quite as acceptable as they did in the good old days. Hockey referee, Peter Friesema, found this to his cost in December 2012, when he was preparing to fly home from Ted Stevens Anchorage International Airport in Alaska following a tournament.

While preparing to board, Friesema noticed that a sticker with his details had been placed on a bag that in fact belonged to his travelling companion. The bag was already trundling away on a conveyor belt when the mistake was noticed.

Freisama was told not to panic.

The sticker didn't matter, an Alaskan Airlines official explained to him, because the bags were all going to the same destination.

"But," cried Freisema (coming up with an instant hilarious joke which might have been better if he'd worked on it for a while), "my friend's bag has a bomb in it!"

A few minutes later, the airport had been evacuated, all flights delayed and everyone waiting was standing outside at midnight in Alaska in the middle of December.

Freisema was questioned by the FBI and arrested on charges of making terroristic threats, a felony, and disorderly conduct.

So, it's true what they say – the secret of great humour is timing. And this had definitely not been the time.

Other similar mistimed "quips" have been recorded at US airports in recent years. These included a man who told officials, "I have eight bombs on me" and another who claimed he had a bomb in his bag because he thought that would help get him through security a bit quicker.

In July 2015, a terror alert was sparked at Glasgow Airport when an X-ray machine picked up the image of an actual explosive device hidden in an item of luggage.

The owner was flying out for his stag do at the time but to get the trip off to a hilarious start, one of his friends had planted the fake bomb in his bag. Well, in the tradition of stag dos, he presumably ended up naked in a back room of the airport having his body intimately searched by a stranger dressed in a uniform.

You therefore have to use Fake News about fake bombs very skilfully if you want to achieve your own ends.

Another unfortunate prospective groom staged a bomb hoax on his own wedding day in Liverpool in 2013. He was not a terrorist or an anarchist. What he was was terrified.

The hapless groom had forgotten to complete the forms needed to get married and was now too frightened to tell his fiancée that their wedding wasn't going to go ahead as planned.

Come the scheduled wedding day, there was clearly nothing for it but to phone the registry office, put on a fake accent and make a hoax bomb threat.

The wedding therefore had to be abandoned and nobody found out what he had done until a few hours later when he was arrested.

If the 12-month prison sentence that resulted from his little hoax was preferable to his fiancée's reaction, she must be a formidable woman.

At least he was safe from her while he was locked up!

TRUMP'S
GREATEST HITS

"THERE ARE TWO KINDS OF TRUTH. THERE ARE REAL
TRUTHS, AND THERE ARE MADE-UP TRUTHS."

— Marion Barry
(US politician and second Mayor of the District of Columbia
— following his arrest for crack cocaine possession)

THE GREATEST
ACHIEVEMENTS OF
DONALD TRUMP 1

PRESIDENT TRUMP INVENTED all the great scientific theories including Einstein's theory of relatives (don't ask President Trump to explain any of them to you though – he is a busy man).

THE GREATEST ACHIEVEMENTS OF DONALD TRUMP 2

PRESIDENT TRUMP WROTE THE complete works of Shakespeare (which is a book with all the best words in it and which everyone thinks is just terrific).

Don't ask the President any detailed questions about the contents of *Donald J Trump's Big Book of All the Plays I Have Written Myself With No Help From Anyone Else* aka *The*

Complete Works of Shakespeare though.

He is a busy man and he can't be expected to remember everything about all the great books that he's written.

Not even the titles. Or what they're about. Or anything really.

That's how busy he is.

Donald Trump ● Follow

To nuke or not to nuke, that is the question...

THE GREATEST ACHIEVEMENTS OF DONALD TRUMP 3

PRESIDENT TRUMP gets the highest ratings whenever he's on TV. That's what it's all about these days. It's no good being President of the United States if you're not getting high ratings.

If you don't get high ratings how would anyone ever know you're even president?

President Trump gets the best ratings of any president ever. They are really terrific ratings.

George Washington got zero ratings. John Adams got zero ratings. Thomas Jefferson got zero ratings.

In fact, all the presidents up to the time of the invention of television got zero ratings.

After that, they got some ratings. But none of them have had ratings like President Trump.

Although apparently President Kennedy got pretty good ratings once during some trip to Dallas. President Trump is carefully considering a similar trip because he knows he will get much, much better ratings.

THE GREATEST ACHIEVEMENTS OF DONALD TRUMP 4

PRESIDENT TRUMP was given the Nobel Prize for being the World's Greatest Guy with All the Best Words and the Highest Ratings and Incredible Hair.

The Nobel committee had never given a Nobel Prize for Hairdressing before but when they saw President Trump they invented it there and then.

It was also the first time in history that the Nobel Prize for Hairdressing had been given to the same person who had been awarded the Nobel Prize for the Best Words and the Nobel Prize for Getting the Highest Ratings.

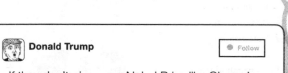

Donald Trump   ● Follow

If they don't give me a Nobel Prize like Obama's, I am going to nuke everyone!

THE GREATEST ACHIEVEMENTS OF DONALD TRUMP 5

PRESIDENT TRUMP was given another Nobel Prize shortly after his Nobel Prizes for Having the Best Words and for Hairdressing.

Overcome by the sight of his magnificent physique, the Nobel Committee invited him to celebrate the award of his Nobel Prizes by making love to all of them in turn.

The Nobel Committee (all of whom I might add were very hot women) were so impressed by his performance that they immediately presented him with the Nobel Prize for Being a Magnificent Lover.

And once they had all finished their lovemaking they all peed on the bed together.

The President of Norway afterwards sent President Trump a bill for the soiled sheets. The President of Norway will surely regret this when a nuclear strike is launched against him.

Then he will really know the meaning of soiled laundry.

THE POWER HANDSHAKE

"THE HONOURABLE MEMBER DID NOT WANT THE TRUTH;
THE HONOURABLE MEMBER HAD ASKED FOR FACTS."

— Joseph Chamberlain

USING A POWER HANDSHAKE TO ASSIST YOUR DISSEMINATION OF FAKE NEWS

PRESIDENT TRUMP is famous for his use of the Power Handshake.

When meeting other world leaders, or just anyone who makes the mistake of offering him their hand, the President will use a special, mysterious and hilarious handshake.

The handshake technique employed by the president will probably have escaped the notice of the casual observer as it is performed in a highly subtle and inconspicuous manner.

Essentially the president will take the extended hand of a person whom he is greeting, grasp it firmly

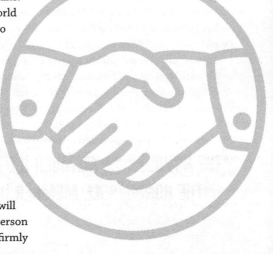

THE POWER HANDSHAKE

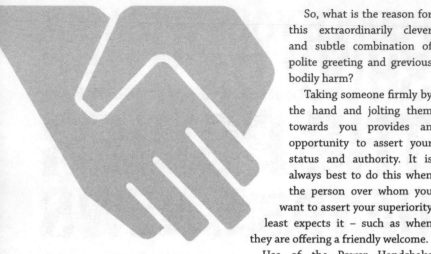

So, what is the reason for this extraordinarily clever and subtle combination of polite greeting and grevious bodily harm?

Taking someone firmly by the hand and jolting them towards you provides an opportunity to assert your status and authority. It is always best to do this when the person over whom you want to assert your superiority least expects it – such as when they are offering a friendly welcome.

Use of the Power Handshake will help convince them of your superior status. It is a well-known psychological fact that nothing makes someone admire you more than the fact you have dislocated their arm.

Once someone is convinced of your superiority they will be sure to believe what you tell them –even if what you tell them is a steaming pile of Fake News.

And if you want to assert yourself even further, you can try kneeing them in the nadgers as you pull them towards yourself.

and then pull it (and possibly the rest of the person to which it is attached) sharply towards himself. Yes, the action may wrench their arm out of its socket in the process but it's their own stupid fault for offering their hand.

This is all done so quickly that it is almost imperceptible to anyone. Although doubters claim evidence for the success of the Power Handshake is circumstantial, it definitely makes an impression. See, for example, the recent photograph of the assembled world leaders at a recent G20 conference which showed that every attendee (apart from Trump and Putin) had ended the gathering with their right arm in a sling.

//

PEOPLE YOU PROBABLY SHOULDN'T USE THE POWER HANDSHAKE ON

- The elderly

- The infirm

- Small children

- People who don't weigh very much, in case you accidentally flip them over your shoulder while shaking hands

- People whose arm is broken

- People with prosthetic limbs that are likely to fly off when jerked towards you

- People with weak joints, in case their actual arm flies off when jerked off

THE POWER HANDSHAKE

- People with no arms at all (forcing them into a humiliating power handshake just looks cruel)

- People in wheelchairs who may be toppled forwards and onto the floor by an overly powerful handshake

- But then again – who cares about these losers! Just jerk them towards you whoever they are!

PEOPLE YOU PROBABLY SHOULDN'T USE THE POWER HANDSHAKE ON – REVISED LIST

- Judo experts (they will use the thrust of the handshake against you and toss you over their shoulder)

- The President of Russia (well-known judo expert)

- People holding sharp implements that are pointing towards you at the time of the handshake (the handshake will very possibly cause them to stab you in the guts)

- People coming towards you at speed in a motor vehicle

- People who you meet who have just been walking their dog and have a small plastic bag of poop in their hand at the time (the bag may explode against the front of your shirt with disastrous consequences)

SWINDLERS
& LOSERS

"I APOLOGISE FOR LYING TO YOU ... I PROMISE I WON'T
DECEIVE YOU EXCEPT IN MATTERS OF THIS SORT."

— Spiro T. Agnew
(US Vice-President, after taking reporters
on a surprise trip to Cambodia in 1970)

FAKE LUCRE –
THE WORLD CLASSIC FINANCIAL SWINDLES

YOU DON'T HAVE TO BE A FAMOUS politician or a rich, powerful and influential guy to come up with Fake News – although it certainly does help.

Some people choose to do things the other way around and make themselves famous and rich through their own clever use of Fake News.

Some people have been so successful at doing this that their names have become associated for all time with criminal financial irregularity. Now that really is fame!

YOU GREAT BIG PONZI

CHARLES PONZI was such a great swindler that he received the ultimate tribute of having a type of fraud named in his honour.

Even better, he didn't actually invent the Ponzi scheme himself! Nevertheless, Ponzi managed to con us all into thinking a financial scam belonged to him when he had in fact nicked the idea from someone else!

Ponzi was born in Italy in 1882 and emigrated to the USA in 1903. He claimed that he managed to gamble his life savings away during the voyage and arrived with only $2.50 in his pocket. What a promising start for a future financial tycoon!

A few years later, Ponzi had settled in Boston where he came up with a scheme to make money based on an odd feature of the postal system.

Letters sent abroad at the time usually included an international reply coupon. This could be swapped by the recipient for the minimum postage required to send a letter back again.

Fluctuations in exchange rates and postal charges meant that it was possible to buy these coupons cheaply in other countries (for example, back home in Italy) and send them to the USA where they could be swapped for stamps that were worth slightly more than the coupons' original purchase price.

Ponzi had agents in Italy send him reply coupons which he used to earn himself a decent income – albeit all in the form of low denomination postage stamps.

Despite this, this scheme worked

so well Ponzi began to find other people who wanted to invest in the scheme with him.

And then he had an idea which was not only brilliant, it was completely illegal!

Ponzi noticed that the money from his postal coupon scheme was coming in fast. In fact, it was coming in so fast that he could afford to pay his older investors the profits they were expecting from the cash being paid in by his ever-increasing number of new investors.

Strictly speaking you didn't really need to bother with all that messing around with coupons and postage stamps at all! It did however provide a convenient cover for a criminal scheme.

The only problem with the Ponzi Scheme was that you either needed to keep finding more and more new investors or you had to talk your old investors out of withdrawing their money.

But as long as you could do that, the plan would work like a dream.

Right up to the point when you went to jail.

Trouble began brewing when a financial journalist called Clarence Barron noticed something unusual about Ponzi's business. Ponzi himself seemed strangely reluctant to invest his own money in his unfailingly profitable enterprise. Instead, he chose to put his cash into boring old-fashioned investments such as real estate, stocks and bonds.

Another tiny clue that Barron spotted was the fact that, even though there were only 27,000 postal reply coupons in the world, Ponzi had acquired so many investors there would have to be 160 million coupons in circulation for them to be turning a profit. Either Ponzi was running the scheme not just on this planet but on

5,925 other worlds, all of which had similar postal systems, or something wasn't quite right.

Barron's exposé was published in the Boston Post in July 1920. People remained reluctant to accept that the scheme into which they had poured their life savings was a scam. On the day the *Boston Post* story published details of the fraud, a queue of new investors lined up outside Ponzi's office desperate to give him their money.

So, remember – if your Fake News sounds good enough, people will continue to believe in it even if it means losing their entire life's savings!

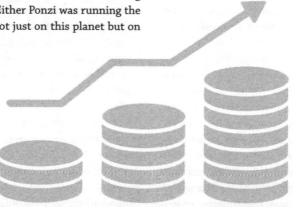

YOU DON'T HAVE TO BE MADOFF TO WORK HERE, BUT IT HELPS

BERNIE MADOFF was responsible for the biggest Ponzi scheme in history. Sadly, despite his hard work and criminal activities, he did not have any type of fraud named after him.

However, his name, as many have noted, was a classic example of nominative determinism. Maybe it should have served as a warning to his hapless investors before Bernie made-off with their cash.

One great Fake News technique that Madoff used to make everyone trust him was the cunning ruse of working as a respected professional financier for several decades.

Madoff started his own firm in 1960 with $5,000 earned from a stint working as a lifeguard. He built it up until it was one of Wall Street's top market maker businesses, helped launch the NASDAQ stock market, served as its chairman in 1990, 1991 and 1993 and was a board member of the National Association of Securities Dealers.

And then he decided that this was all fine and good but what he really wanted to do was get into financial

A-List Hollywood stars including Steven Spielberg, Kevin Bacon, Zsa Zsa Gabor, John Malkovich and even the estate of the late John Denver.

Madoff was no snob however and went out of his way to trick much less wealthy customers including the elderly as well as charities such as the Elie Wiesel Foundation for Humanity into investing their money in his fraudulent scheme.

And then the 2008 financial crash happened. This meant less new investors could be found and more old investors wanted to get their hands on their cash.

Madoff's clients requested $7 billion in returns. Madoff found he only had around $200 million to $300 million to offer them.

irregularity on the biggest scale anyone had ever seen.

In December 2008, Madoff allegedly confessed to his employees that the asset management side of his business was in fact a massive Ponzi scheme. Older clients were being paid, using money from new clients rather than from any profits made on their investments.

At the same time, more and more new clients were being tempted in by the money made by the old clients.

And what's more, his clients were

Madoff had managed to accumulate $17 billion in actual losses and $65 billion in paper losses (in other words the earnings that his clients could have made if they had invested their money elsewhere).

In 2011, he was jailed for 150 years which should take him until he is 221. Tragically, his two sons both died since his arrest. Mark Madoff committed suicide on the second anniversary of his father's arrest while Andrew Madoff died of cancer four years later.

LUSTIG FOR LIFE

COUNT VICTOR LUSTIG was born in 1890 in Austria. Or was he?

This name was just one of 47 aliases that the con artist known as Count Victor Lustig used during his career. When this individual ended up in Alcatraz Prison, another of his many names was used on his documentation – Robert V. Miller.

To this day nobody is sure who he really was. So, this guy was getting away with Fake News from the moment they filled in his birth certificate – presumably with all 47 of his aliases listed in the "name of child" box.

One of Lustig's greatest cons was a "money printing machine". This was a wooden box with rollers and dials which would produce a perfect copy of a $100 bill. The machine did this using the recently discovered wonder element radium. Unfortunately, such was the quality of the reproduction that it took six hours to copy each $100 bill.

Lustig's box tended to work exactly three times. It did this once to demonstrate the accuracy of the $100 bills it could produce.

At this stage, the person watching the demonstration would think, "This machine can produce $100 every 6 hours! That's $400 a day!"

Lustig would then be talked into selling his miracle machine for $30,000. This was a lot of money but, at $400 a day, it would pay for itself in 75 days.

What they didn't think was that while they were watching a wooden box print out a $100 dollar note over a 6-hour period, Lustig had plenty of time to get as far away as possible.

After printing two more $100 bills, the box would then just produce blank pieces of paper. It must have been a bit like the experience of trying out an ink cartridge computer printer.

The client would then realize they had just paid $30,000 for a small wooden box that had been pre-loaded with three genuine $100 bills.

In 1925, Lustig visited Paris armed with documents carrying the official seal of the French government. He based himself at the Hotel de Crillon on the Place de la Concorde and from

there contacted the leading scrap metal merchants in France.

He was, he informed them, a representative of the French government who had responsibility for the scrappage of a large metal structure in the middle of Paris. There was quite a lot of metal to be scrapped because the structure in question was quite large and rather noticeable on the Paris skyline. It was Gustave Eiffel's Tower.

At the time, the tower was only 36-years-old and had not originally been intended as a permanent structure. it was now getting a little old, rusty and expensive to maintain and so the decision had been made to dispose of it. Obviously, this couldn't be announced publicly because the people of Paris would become a little upset as a result.

Andre Poisson was the lucky scrap metal merchant selected to handle the scrapping of the tower. But there was one condition. Lustig explained that as he was a poorly paid civil servant, a sizeable backhander would be needed to secure the deal for Poisson. When the money was provided, Lustig skipped town. It is believed he proceeded to play the same trick on a series of other hapless scrap metal dealers.

It's a wonder the Eiffel Tower is still there today!

VICTOR LUSTIG'S 10 COMMANDMENTS FOR CONMEN

IF YOU WANT TO GET AWAY with Fake News, there is no better set of rules to follow than those attributed to Count Victor Lustig.

Lustig was reputed to be the author a series of instructions for conning people. Possibly someone else was really the author. But if so, that's yet another con that Lustig got away with:

- Be a patient listener (it is this, not fast talking, that gets a con man his coups)

- Never look bored

- Wait for the other person to reveal any political opinions, then agree with them

- Let the other person reveal religious views, then have the same ones

- Hint at sex talk, but don't follow it up unless the other person shows a strong interest

- Never discuss illness, unless some special concern is shown

- Never pry into a person's personal circumstances (they'll tell you all eventually)

- Never boast – just let your importance be quietly obvious

- Never be untidy

- Never get drunk

REIS A BIT OF CASH

LIKE CHARLES PONZI AND COUNT VICTOR LUSTIG, ARTUR VIRGÍLIO ALVES REIS was another financial Fake News merchant born in Europe towards the end of the 19th century.

Conmen today must regard this period as being monetary fraud's equivalent of the Renaissance

As a budding fraudster Reis' speciality was forgery. He had excellent educational qualifications. Well, he had forged his diploma from Oxford University.

And using these credentials he got a job as an official railway inspector in Portuguese Angola. Here he did a bit more forgery to produce cheques of sufficient value to take control of Ambaca, the Royal Trans-African Railway Company of Angola.

Luckily, Reis then found there was sufficient money in Ambaca's coffers to cover the cheques he had forged before they bounced. (NB. this is not how business acquirements are meant to work!)

And, indeed, a court did not regard this as a legitimate way for Reis to advance himself in business. The Oxford educated controller of the Royal Trans-African Railway Company of Angola was therefore sent to prison. He was 26 at the time.

While in jail, Reis hit upon a fabulous new idea for a scam. Why bother forging banknotes when you can just forge documents that will trick a legitimate banknote printer into churning out a massive amount of currency for you?

Again, Reis must have thought, "Where's the crime?"

The con involved presenting Waterlow and Sons, a London based printer of banknotes, with documentation supposedly from Banco de Portugal authorizing the production of 10,000 banknotes each of 500 escudos value.

These were needed to help save Portugal's then colony Angola from its current monetary difficulties. Obviously, the matter had to be kept hush-hush to avoid any further Angolan financial panic.

Waterlow and Sons' printing costs for the job was $7,200. It wasn't cheap. But on the plus side Reis had got five million escudos in return. An instant 70,000 per cent profit!

Presumably, however, Reis did not on this occasion try to pay Waterlow and Sons using the banknotes which they themselves had just printed.

The scam was so irresistible that Reis went back for more and by the end of 1925 had introduced banknotes into the Portuguese economy equivalent to 100 million escudos. Or, to put it another way, he had illegally printed banknotes equivalent to 0.88

per cent of Portuguese total GDP at the time.

When the fraud was discovered, the Banco de Portugal had to withdraw every single 500-escudo note from circulation.

The resulting loss of confidence in the Portuguese government led to its overthrow in a military coup in May 1926 and ultimately to the authoritarian government of António de Oliveira Salazar, which endured until 1968.

As for Reis, he was swiftly sent back to prison in December 1925. He had achieved this monumental damage to the Portuguese government and economy in just 15 months since he had been released from jail following the Ambaca affair!

THE BEST WORDS

"I ALWAYS TELL THE TRUTH. EVEN WHEN I LIE."

– Al Pacino

PRESIDENT TRUMP'S BEST WORDS

IN DECEMBER 2015, when running as presidential candidate, Donald Trump told a rally in South Carolina, "I know words. I have the best words."

This was a proud and incontrovertible boast. It was because he had the best words that Trump triumphed over other candidates who had no words at all and was able to run rings round the candidates who had some words but not the best words. These guys only had words like "Uh", "Dude" and "Shucks". Few of the candidates who only had words of this quality made it to the later stages of the presidential contest.

So, here are some of President Trump's best words:

"BIGLY"

In May 2016, Trump announced that he would win the Presidential race bigly. And indeedly he didly. He went on to announce in his first presidential debate with Hillary Clinton: "I'm going to cut taxes bigly, and you're going to raise taxes bigly." Some linguistic experts (including the president's son Eric Trump) have claimed that he is not saying "bigly" but "big league". Either way he's contributed great new words, bigly.

"SCHLONGED"

In December 2015, Trump said that Hillary Clinton "got schlonged" by Barack Obama in the 2008 presidential race. Many linguistic experts pointed out that "schlong" is a vulgar expression for a man's willy. But then linguistic experts are notorious for having filthy minds. Trump tweeted angrily, "When I said that Hillary Clinton got schlonged by Obama, it meant got beaten badly. The media knows this. Often used word in politics!" No, it wasn't – although it is now!

GET ME A *YU-UGE* COVFEFE AND MAKE IT BIGLY!

"YU-UGE"

In Trump's world things are not just huge. They are *yu-uge*. Not only is *yu-uge* huger than huge, it's the noise made when passing a particularly large bowel movement. And after an extra-large bucket of Trump's favourite dinner, chicken nuggets, you know that really will be *yu-uge*.

"COVFEFE"

One of Trump's best words ever. No one had even heard it before Trump tweeted in May 2017, "Despite all the press covfefe..." He then possibly slumped into unconsciousness mid-tweet. Or maybe he was distracted by doing some great government work. By the next morning everyone was talking about covfefe. Nobody knew what it was but people were printing it on hats, caps and covfefe mugs. You see how great President Trump is? He created American jobs with just one word that no one had ever thought of before. Not even Shakespeare, all of whose works were of course, as we established earlier, written by Donald Trump.

"LEIGHTWEIGHT CHOCKER"

In February 2016, Trump described Florida senator Marco Rubio as "a leightweight chocker". People thought it was a misspelling. It is never a misspelling. It is more exciting new words. The best words. Trump not only creates jobs, he creates entire new words. By the end of his presidency we will all be talking a brand-new language. President Trump is not only creating jobs for American miners, he is creating jobs for the people who write American dictionaries!

TRUMP FANS

> "EIGHT MORE DAYS AND I CAN START TELLING THE TRUTH AGAIN!"
> — Chris Dodd
> (US Senator during a political campaign)

PEOPLE WHO HAVE MET PRESIDENT DONALD TRUMP AND WHO THINK HE IS JUST GREAT – NUMBER 1

TH*R*S* M*Y – PR*M* M*N*ST*R OF THE UN*T*D K*NGD*M

"President Trump had to hold my hand when I met him in Washington in January 2017 shortly after his inauguration. He had to grab me by the hand because – like all women who meet this great man – I had come over all peculiar in his presence. In order to save me from falling the ground at the sight of this Adonis, President Trump showed himself a true gentleman by grabbing by the hand, and not grabbing me by anything else because I was an elderly and therefore grotesque looking woman only 20 years his junior. What a specimen of masculinity he is. Unfortunately, there is no chance of romance between us because (as he told me himself in a very gentle and considerate manner) I am so very hideously old and deeply unattractive. Oh, if only I were a woman 30 years younger than I currently am rather than an ugly old bag barely 20 years younger than President Trump."

 Donald Trump [Follow]

Dear Theresa, you looked really grey when I met you. It was like you'd just seen something horrific.

PEOPLE WHO HAVE MET PRESIDENT DONALD TRUMP AND WHO THINK HE IS JUST GREAT – NUMBER 2

THE P*PE

"Usually I am a happy soul. I looked a little glum in the photos that were taken when Donald Trump came to see me in May 2017. But that was just because meeting this great man had made me realize how worthless and empty of meaning my life had been. I had achieved absolutely nothing compared to this guy. OK, I had got to be Pope and spiritual leader to billions around the world. But that seems like nothing to me now."

 Donald Trump

Hi Pope! I think you're just great. Particularly your early work with Snap and Crackle.

PEOPLE WHO HAVE MET PRESIDENT DONALD TRUMP AND WHO THINK HE IS JUST GREAT – NUMBER 3

A*GE*A M*RK*L – CH*NC*LL*R OF G*RM*NY

"I looked quite solemn when I met President Trump in March 2017. I sat there simply begging him to shake my hand while photographers from the World's Fake News Mainstream Media outlets were taking photos of us. President Trump of course knew the devastating effect that physical contact with him would have on any woman – let alone a hideous old bag like me. And so, like a true gentleman, he refused to shake my hand and sat there failing to heed my pathetic requests. Instead, he sat there as though I didn't exist at all. And this just made me respect him all the more. Our meeting went just great. I don't care what anyone else says."

Donald Trump   ⬤ Follow

Angela Merkel, you know nothing. You think your name is pronounced Angular.

PEOPLE WHO HAVE MET
PRESIDENT DONALD TRUMP
AND WHO THINK HE IS
JUST GREAT – NUMBER 4

B*R*CK OB*MA
– FORMER (AND LESS GOOD)
PR*S*D*NT OF THE UN*T*D
ST*T*S OF A**R*C*

"I looked quite solemn when I was photographed meeting Donald Trump before he became President. This was because he had just explained to me in painstaking detail what a worthless human being and illegitimate president I had been. And do you know what, he was absolutely right. I have learnt everything I know about being Pr*s*d*nt of the Un*t*d St*t*s from Donald Trump. Unfortunately, it was too late because by then I had already been president and done it all wrong. That was the main reason he had to become president after me. To show me how I had done it all wrong. I studied everything he did to learn how the job should have been done. I even tried to tape him (as he correctly said) through his microwave oven. As a result I have been able to follow the same diet of instant ready meals that he eats. I can only apologize to the American people for having done being president wrong. It turns out I didn't even get the bit about which country you had to be born in right and had forged my own birth certificate to show I was born in the USA and not – as is obviously the case – in Africa. President Trump has however graciously chosen not to prosecute me for this crime as I was only a baby at the time when I did it."

Donald Trump Follow

What a disastrous president. Not my words.
His – when he met me.

Donald Trump

Follow

My pal Nigel takes great selfies. Pity he always makes the mistake of being in them himself though.

PEOPLE WHO HAVE MET
PRESIDENT DONALD TRUMP
AND WHO THINK HE IS
JUST GREAT – NUMBER 5

N*G*L F*R*G*
– F*RM*R L*ADE*R OF UKI*

"I did not look at all solemn when I met Donald Trump. That is because I am one of his greatest pals. He really likes me. I can tell because whenever he sees me he simply wees himself laughing. Then he told the British Prime Minister they should make me the UK's ambassador to Washington. And then he laughed and wee'd himself a bit more. It's fantastic to be able to make someone so happy. Mind you, he is getting a bit old so for all I know he pees himself on a regular basis. Speaking of which I heard a rumour about some Russian chappy who is pursuing him for recompense because some of his hotel bed sheets got ruined. But that's all probably just evil tittle tattle and locker room banter. Once I met Donald Trump in one of the golden lifts in Trump Tower. Luckily, I managed to get a picture of the two of us together. Once again, he was laughing hysterically. Possibly this was because he was just thinking of having his bodyguards throw me out onto the street. I was just pleased to make him so happy. What a guy!"

EXPERTS

"I DON'T WANT ANY YES-MEN AROUND ME.
I WANT EVERYBODY TO TELL ME THE TRUTH, EVEN IF IT
COSTS THEM THEIR JOBS."

— Samuel Goldwyn

WHAT IS AN EXPERT? AND WHY DON'T WE NEED THEM ANY MORE?

A **WISE MAN ONCE SAID,** "People in this country have had enough of experts."

But who exactly are these experts? And why does anyone pay attention to this elitist group of bespectacled no-hopers?

Experts are a particular problem to all those of us interested in using Fake News for fun and profit.

This is because experts know lots of stuff – and none of it is fake. Experts will therefore be quick to point out if you say anything wrong. Even worse, they will be quick to provide detailed evidence why you're wrong and to exactly what degree. Experts are therefore the sworn enemies of all Fake News merchants.

An expert is someone who is professionally employed to tell the rest of us that we are wrong about all manner of things. An expert will tell us that what we think about stuff is based on false assumptions and a lack of proper information.

The Mainstream Media will frequently make use of "experts" in an effort to make out that the stuff that normal people like us say is ill-informed and ignorant.

This is an outrage!

Why should these experts be allowed to treat us like this just because we don't really know what we're talking about? Do our ill-thought-out, gut reactions to issues we know nothing about and which we have never previously considered in our lives count for nothing?

That's why today people don't want experts any more. Instead, they prefer Fake News merchants who pretend to be experts!

 Donald Trump [Follow]

Experts! What the hell do they know?

REASONS WHY FAKE NEWS MERCHANTS ARE BETTER THAN EXPERTS

XPERTS ARE VERY BORING PEOPLE. An expert will know so much about the thing they are an expert on that they will be able to go on and on about it.

Experts will go on and on about their subject in extreme detail – almost as though they were experts.

The things that experts are expert in are themselves very, very boring things, like science, history and the arts, that no one in their right mind could ever be interested enough in to become an expert.

Experts are very elitist who will be sniffy about certain subjects.

Experts are very rude. Experts will tell you that if you are an expert on a subject such as the contents of your own bellybutton or the activities of your immediate neighbours, this is not a proper subject for expertise.

Because experts know so much, they are completely inflexible with their knowledge.

Experts do not understand the importance of telling people what they want to hear regardless of the facts.

Unlike experts, professional Fake News merchants are always happy to tell people what they want to hear.

Professional Fake News merchants will make the things they say sound like expertise even though they have adapted the facts or made it all up like a skilled craftsman.

Fake News merchants never have any problem looking knowledgeable because they are very good at cheating.

Fake News merchants have access to the Internet – give a Fake News merchants five minutes and access to Google and they will be able to make themselves an expert on any subject of your choosing.

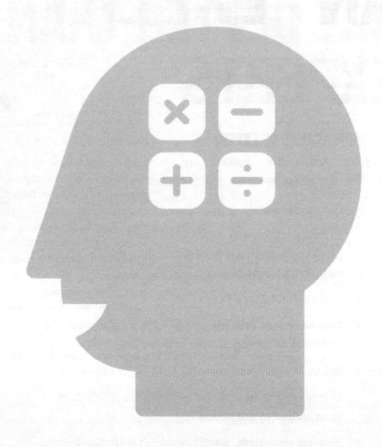

///

HOW TO SPOT AN "EXPERT"

How can you spot one of these experts? Here are the tell-tale signs to watch out for:

APPEARANCE OF EXPERT

- Will probably be wearing glasses

- Sticky out ears

- Build-up of ear wax in ears, which will be particularly noticeable because ears are sticking out facing towards you

- Prominent Adam's apple

- Bad haircut held in place with grease (possibly naturally occurring and of own making)

- Warts in various places

- Under weight, as a result of being too interested in expertise to eat properly

- Sloping shoulders, each piled high with dandruff

CLOTHING WORN BY EXPERT

- Will generally be unfashionable
- Lab coat
- Tank top
- Row of pens in breast pocket
- Will be wearing tie (probably woollen)

NOTICEABLE ODOURS COMING FROM EXPERT

- Smell of nasal decongestant
- Smell of urine and faeces from trousers
- Chemicals from laboratory work

SEX OF EXPERT

- Very unlikely

GENDER OF EXPERT

- Almost certainly male but basically neutral

SCIENTIFIC EQUIPMENT LIKELY TO BE USED BY EXPERT

- Calculator constantly at hand
- Will know what the calculator buttons that no one else ever uses do
- Slide rule
- Will know what a slide rule is for
- Set of test tubes and a Bunsen Burner

FINANCIAL SITUATION OF EXPERT

- Will be poorly paid
- Will mainly be interested in government grants available for research
- Will also be knowledgeable in the cost of advanced equipment such as really big, state of the art calculators and test tubes

EXPERTISE OF EXPERT

- Theoretically extensive (he is an expert after all)
- But unintelligible to ordinary people and therefore effectively worthless

FAKE
SCIENCE

"HALF THE LIES OUR OPPONENTS TELL
ABOUT US ARE UNTRUE."

– Sir Boyle Roche

FAKE NEWS SCIENTISTS – DODGY CLAIMS IN THE WORLD OF SCIENCE

SCIENCE IS A DISCIPLINE that is meant to be entirely based on observable facts. This puts Fake News enthusiasts who choose to work in the field of science at a very unfair disadvantage.

Despite this, some great individuals achieve significant success in deceiving their fellow scientists, not to mention the idiots in the wider population who will believe anything.

These scientific Fake News merchants deserve our respect and commendation for their achievements in the face of not only the scientific establishment but the physical laws of the universe.

DAWSON AROUND – FAKE FOSSILS

IN 1859 CHARLES DARWIN published *On the Origin of Species*. This work laid out the theory of evolution by natural selection and the idea that all the creatures running around today evolved from earlier, simpler life forms.

Some have tried to show that Darwin's theory was itself a nasty hoax and that the Earth was in fact created by God on October 23, 4004 BC, as John Ussher a 17th century Archbishop of Ireland calculated based on the *Bible*.

This date seems oddly specific and would mean that the Earth shares its birthday with Ryan Reynolds, Brazilian footballing legend Pelé and Weird Al Yankovic.

Others however have worked to find evidence to back up Darwin's theory. And at least one of these did so by means of a highly successful piece of Fake News.

Although he skirted around the issue in *On the Origin of Species*, the theory of evolution pointed to a disturbing conclusion for Darwin's fellow Victorians. Like all other creatures on Earth, we humans must also have come from earlier, simpler life forms. Well, we all have some relatives like that.

In the years after Darwin, the hunt was on for the missing link or, as biologists call it, the "last common ancestor" between ourselves and other primates alive today.

Annoyingly, the most important discoveries of ancient human remains were being found on the continent. In 1907, a 500,000-year-old human-like jawbone was found in Heidelberg, Germany.

Charles Dawson was an amateur archaeologist based in Sussex. Obviously, having a name that was a little bit like Charles Darwin meant that you were sure to have a similarly revolutionary impact on evolutionary science.

And so it turned out!

Dawson discovered several apparently important fossils including three new species of dinosaur (one of which, *iguanodon dawsoni*, was named in his honour), teeth from a previously unknown type of mammal (named *plagiaulax dawsoni* in his honour) and a previously unknown fossilized plant (named *salaginella dawsoni* in his honour).

With three new types of dinosaur, a new mammal and a new plant to his credit, Dawson was doing pretty well as a fossil hunter. If only he could find

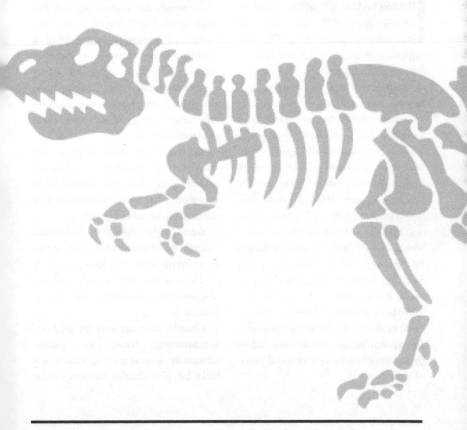

the missing link between apes and humans that had been suggested by Darwin's theory.

And then he did.

And by extreme good fortune he found it buried not very far from where he lived in Sussex!

Piltdown is a group of hamlets in East Sussex, south of Ashdown Forest and just off the A272 to Haywards Heath. Here in 1912 Dawson found the missing link – remains of a creature that had a human-like skull with an ape-like jaw.

In fact, what Dawson had found – while presumably desperate to have yet another fossil named in his honour – were two entirely separate things that he himself had planted: a human-like skull from a human-like human; and an ape-like jaw from an ape-like ape.

Working with Arthur Smith Woodward, Keeper of Geology from the Natural History Museum, Dawson went on to uncover more remains from his creature.

These were unveiled at a meeting of the Geological Society in London and said to belong to a 500,000-year-old human ancestor which would satisfyingly be named *eoanthropus dawsoni* or "Dawson's dawn-man". Presumably it was called this because Dawson had got up at dawn to bury the forged remains so he could dig them up later in front of his mate Mr Woodward.

Luckily, nobody from the Natural History Museum bothered to investigate Dawson too closely.

If they had, they might have discovered that he had purchased a skull without a jawbone in 1907 and then asked a local chemist how you would treat a bone to make it look like a fossil.

Dawson's hoax was not exposed however until 1953 and only finally pinned on Dawson himself in recent years.

But by this time the Piltdown perpetrator was, of course, long-gone and was presumably in the process of turning into a fossil himself.

The hoax had wasted scientists' time for over 50 years. Dawson is now unlikely to have any more discoveries named in his honour.

MER-MADE IN JAPAN

A FEW YEARS BEFORE THE Piltdown Man drama, the public were gripped by another extraordinary piece of Fake News concerning a creature made from different parts jammed together.

In the 1840s, the then up-and-coming American showman P. T. Barnum leased a mermaid from its owner Moses Kimball of the Boston Museum for $12.50 a week.

The going rate for mermaids at the time may was considerably higher – but Kimball's specimen was not a very good looking one.

This mermaid was not a beautiful young girl with long flowing blonde hair and a fish's tail. Instead, it was described by Barnum it as "an ugly, dried-up, black-looking, diminutive specimen, about three-feet long."

All in all, the creature resembled the top half of a monkey sewn onto the tail of a large fish. And there was probably quite a good reason why it looked like that!

The mermaid was of course quite dead and appeared to have passed away, as Barnum himself said, "in great agony." But then you would look in some discomfort if someone had sawn you in half and sewed you onto the back end of a fish.

The creature had possibly been acquired some 30 years earlier by Dutch merchants who were then the only westerners permitted to trade with the Japanese.

An American sea captain bought the mermaid from the Dutch,

reportedly paying $6,000 for it. This was quite a lot of money and the captain had to raise funds by selling his ship.

Unfortunately, it then turned out he wasn't the sole owner of the vessel. But never mind – he was now the proud possessor of a genuine mermaid!

The captain came to London and asked some experts to check his mermaid was genuine. When they deemed it to be a fake, he found some other experts whose verdict was more satisfactory.

He exhibited the mermaid in London for a shilling a view but was then sued by the co-owner of his ship, as a result of which the mermaid became a ward of court.

One reason why the $6,000 the captain paid might have been a bit steep is that these mermaids weren't that rare.

Japanese sideshow carnivals, or *misemono*, of the time regularly

//

featured similarly supine mermaids all of which looked suspiciously like dogs or monkeys that had been fitted with fish's tails.

In the Japanese fishermen's defence, belief in mermaids, or *ningyo*, was part of their culture. But they found the genuine article a little difficult to catch. And so, it was easier to make fake ones.

Many westerners saw these Japanese mermaids during the 19th century. Usually their response was not to drum up $6,000 to buy them but rather to admire the skill required to stick two creatures together.

In his 1866 book *Curiosities of Natural History*, Francis Trevelyan Buckland quotes one witness of a Japanese mermaid:

"Captain Cuming, R.N., of Braidwood Terrace, Plymouth, has returned from Yokohama, bringing with him a great variety of curiosities. Amongst them is a mermaid. The head is that of a small monkey, with prominent teeth; a little thin wool on the head and upper parts; long attenuated arms and claws, below which the ribs show very distinctly; beyond these latter the skin of a fish is so neatly joined that it is hardly possible to detect where the fish begins and the monkey leaves off."

Barnum avoided the mistake of calling in experts or exhibiting the mermaid to too many people at once.

Instead, he slowly built up interest by writing to newspapers using a variety of pseudonyms, making mention of the mermaid.

Barnum arranged for the supposed owner of the mermaid to turn up at a hotel in Philadelphia. Here the owner allowed the hotel landlord to have a peak at the creature as a special treat.

The landlord in turn begged for some of his friends to be allowed to come and see this fish tailed wonder. And so, word of the mermaid spread until Barnum exhibited it to a small audience at a New York concert hall for five days. After this it was moved to Barnum's own American museum where crowds flocked to see it.

So, if you have a piece of Fake News which isn't going to stand up to too much scrutiny, the best thing is to slowly dribble out information to a few people at a time until word spreads and you can rake in the profits!

GOING THROUGH THE PERPETUAL MOTIONS

THE PROBLEMS OF LETTING PEOPLE EXAMINE YOUR FAKE NEWS too closely are again demonstrated by the story of Charles Redheffer and his perpetual motion machine.

Today people argue about global warming and the effects caused by burning fossil fuels. Many have described such fears as Fake News but whether they are or not, there should be no need for worry because the world's energy problems were cracked over 200 years ago by American inventor, Charles Redheffer.

Redheffer developed a perpetual motion machine which he first exhibited it in Philadelphia in 1812. In case you're wondering what a perpetual motion machine might look like – it was made of wood and had various wheels and cogs that span under the force of a couple of delicately positioned weights.

And in case you're wondering if a perpetual motion machine might actually work – no it won't. Don't blame me – blame the laws of thermodynamics!

However, Redheffer's machine seemingly required no power to operate and yet was capable of running another device attached alongside it via a series of gears. Fantastic! Endless free power!

You would think that the creation of a perpetual motion machine would guarantee its inventor a fortune. Redheffer for some reason however felt the need to charge members of the public to come and see his device working.

An application was also made to the governors of Philadelphia for a bit of cash to help build a larger version of the contraption.

Obviously, Redheffer didn't allow the city's representatives to look too closely at his perpetual motion machine. Doing so would be disastrous to its workings. It was therefore

important that they stood back a little way. Behind a barred window. Far enough away so they couldn't quite see how it worked.

They did, however, notice something odd about the gears connecting it to the device it was being used to power. The gears were worn as though the power was coming not from the perpetual motion machine but from the other direction. It was as though the device that the perpetual motion machine was turning was in fact the thing that was powering the perpetual motion machine!

The city inspectors built their own version of the machine to demonstrate what they thought was going on. This must have been fairly accurate because Redheffer immediately skipped town. Presumably he did not rely on the power of his perpetual motion machine to do so.

Redheffer then attempted the same scam in New York.

Here, a mechanical engineer called Robert Fulton spotted that Redheffer's device was wobbling. It was as though it was being powered by a hidden hand-crank.

Money was offered in return for an investigation and Redheffer found himself powerless to refuse.

After panels were stripped from the wall behind the machine, it turned out to be connected, by a length of catgut, to a room above where an old bearded man was discovered turning a handle to power the machine while eating a crust of bread with his free hand.

Well, it's a sort of perpetual motion, isn't it? You just have to be able to find enough old bearded men and lock them in an upstairs room with enough bread.

A little while later, Redheffer claimed to have constructed yet another machine. And this time it really worked! Redheffer had obviously learnt his lesson now and was reluctant to let anyone see it at all.

Presumably, it's still out there today working away perpetually, possibly with an old man in a room above eagerly awaiting his next delivery of crusts.

THE SECRET OF
ETERNAL FAKE NEWS

ONE VITAL PRINCIPLE of successful Fake News is to tell people that you have discovered a secret that everyone wants. This might be perpetual motion or it could be the secret of immortality.

Obviously, there is no problem with achieving the secret of immortality. All you have to do is stay alive long enough until someone discovers it. And in 18th-century Europe everyone must have thought they had managed to do exactly this.

German physician Johann Heinrich Cohausen detailed the secret of eternal life in *Hermippus Redivivus,* published in 1742. Cohausen was 77 at the time, so perhaps he thought he had genuinely cracked it.

The *Hermippus Redivivus* told you how you could extend your life indefinitely. All you needed to do was consume an elixir formed from the breath of young ladies collected in bottles. Presumably, Cohausen meant you should collect the young ladies' breath in the bottles rather than the young ladies themselves. These days if you tried doing this, the elixir of eternal life would presumably whiff of stale alcopops and Haribos.

At the conclusion of *Hermippus Redivivus*, the author let slip that the work was a satire and not meant to be taken entirely seriously.

Cohausen emphasized that he hadn't really discovered the secret of eternal life by dying in 1750.

THERE'S GOLD IN THEM THERE OCEANS!

ANOTHER THING JUST ABOUT EVERYONE WANTS IS A HOARD OF CASH. As we have seen, get-rich-quick schemes are always successful – at least as far as Fake News goes.

So, it is good news that millions of pounds of gold can be found floating around in seawater all over the world. The bad news is that you have to dredge through a heck of a lot of seawater to find it!

It is estimated that about 20 million pounds of gold is suspended throughout the world's oceans. That means that one litre of seawater might contain 13 billionths of a gram of gold. There is therefore little use taking a bucket-full to one of those shops that promise to buy gold.

Nevertheless, two men in Passamaquoddy Bay, Maine, claimed to have solved the problem.

In 1897, Prescott Ford Jernegan, a Baptist minister, and Charles W Fisher, an experienced diver,

FAKE SCIENCE

presented a jeweller called Arthur Ryan with their "gold accumulator". The accumulator was a box which could harvest gold from seawater using a process involving mercury and electricity and which had been revealed to Jernegan in a divine vision. Well, he was a clergyman, so it must be true!

Ryan being a canny man insisted on seeing the accumulator in action at a site of his own choosing.

The box was taken, lowered into the sea and retrieved a few hours later. Amazingly, when the box was pulled out of the water, it was found to have worked. The box was now covered in bits of gold.

Sadly, this was the only occasion when it would ever work.

Nevertheless, impressed with this one successful demonstration, Ryan and other investors paid $350,000 to establish the "Electrolytic Marine Salts Company" and handed Jernegan and Fisher $200,000 each for their services.

The investors might have done better to consider exactly what mix of skills had brought a clergyman and his deep-sea diving friend together in this enterprise. Fisher had indeed swum down to the accumulator during the test and filled it with pieces of gold.

Once the Electrolytic Marine Salts Company was up and running, no further gold seemed to be harvested. When the investors went to find out what was going on, they discovered that Fisher had disappeared. But then deep-sea divers are good at that.

The Reverend Jernegan promised to go and find what had happened to his friend and then promptly vanished himself. Later, he re-appeared in the Philippines where he was working as a teacher and, possibly overcome with Christian contrition, he refunded $75,000 of his investors' stolen money.

THEY DON'T LIKE IT UPAS THEM!

IF YOU CAN'T GET AWAY WITH fraudulent inventions or discoveries, why not try some scientific Fake News about something that should be impossible for anyone to go and check?

The legend of the Upas, the world's most deadly tree, took hold in the late 18th century when a report was published in *The London Magazine*. An account by a Dutch surgeon described a tree on the island of Java that was so toxic it killed every living thing within a 15-mile radius.

No one managed to explain exactly who had discovered this serial killing tree or how they had survived to carry the news back to London.

Had someone sat watching this tree through an extraordinarily powerful telescope? Did they notice that every time someone crossed a line 15 miles from it they would instantly drop dead? That would mean that if an Upas tree were planted in the middle of Trafalgar Square, everyone would die as soon as they passed the M25!

Some brave soul nevertheless went to check just how deadly the Upas tree was. It turned out that it did indeed produce a poisonous latex which was traditionally used on arrowheads. But it was unlikely to kill you if you were a good five hours' walk away.

The Upas also turned to be a member of the mulberry and fig family – which doesn't sound quite so terrifying!

FAKE MY LIFE

"IT IS NOT FAIR TO SAY THAT I HAVE MISINFORMED CONGRESS OR OTHER CABINET OFFICERS. I HAVEN'T TESTIFIED TO THAT. I'VE TESTIFIED THAT I WITHHELD INFORMATION FROM CONGRESS. AND WITH REGARD TO THE CABINET OFFICERS, I DIDN'T WITHHOLD ANYTHING FROM THEM THAT THEY DIDN'T WANT WITHHELD FROM THEM."

– John Poindexter
(US Rear Admiral, testifying regarding
the Iran-Contra affair)

USING FAKE NEWS IN YOUR OWN PATHETIC LIFE

BY THIS STAGE YOU ARE NO DOUBT THINKING, "This idea of lying in an insane and reckless manner every hour of the waking day sounds great! But what if I'm not a multi-billionaire and/or the (dubiously) elected head of a large and very powerful country? Can I still enjoy the benefits that come with using Fake News?"

It is, of course, an advantage to the Fake News enthusiast if he or she happens to be disgustingly wealthy.

Before you begin your career in Fake News it may, therefore, be best to try and make yourself filthy rich. People will believe anything you tell them if you are swimming in spondoolicks. This may be because they are mesmerized by the sight of you. Or perhaps because they think you are so successful, you must always know what you're talking about. Or it may be because they are trying to work how an idiot like you made so much money. Or it could just be that they have to go along with everything you say because they depend on you for continued employment and are terrified of losing their job.

All these things make Fake News much easier. Some might say almost too easy!

But you can practice Fake News whoever you are. Even if you are living on benefits. In fact, Fake News might help you get a few extra benefits to which you might not be strictly entitled.

Or you can just get your career in Fake News started by telling people you're worth a mint when in fact you've got an overdraft of several million!

USING FAKE NEWS IN YOUR OWN LIFE – WHAT YOU WILL NEED

1. A MASSIVE EGO

This is the first thing you will need to become a successful creator and purveyor of Fake News. Without an ego the size of a planet, you might worry that people would regard you as a deluded, mentally unstable compulsive liar. With a massive ego, you can make up Fake News to your heart's delight and not give a stuff what anyone else thinks.

Of course, as many people know, I (not President Trump, remember) am a truly humble man. Luckily, however I have an enormous ego that helps make up for it. In fact, my ego has been professionally measured by trained psychiatrists and they have shown it to be probably the biggest and best ego that anyone has ever had.

Very few people would be able to manage having such an enormous ego as mine but I seem to manage it just fine. In fact, I find it useful to have such a colossal ego. Without it I probably wouldn't be able to appreciate just how great I am. Or how humble. Yes, I am possibly one of the greatest humble men who ever lived.

So, having a massive ego is probably the best thing that has ever happened to me – or to anyone else for that matter. Sometimes I like to sit and think what Jesus could have done if he'd had my ego!

FAKE MY LIFE

Donald Trump `Follow`

I won the award for being the world's most humble man ever. I presented it to myself.

2. A TOTAL LACK OF SHAME

As well as having probably the biggest and best ego in history, people also tell me that I have no shame. Again, this is a great advantage for a creator of Fake News. It might be a drawback if I didn't have a massive ego and wasn't completely great. But, of course, because I am so such a truly fantastic guy there is no need for any sense of shame. What should I feel ashamed about? It would be a total waste of time. Without shame, you can say and do whatever the heck you feel like and everyone else just has to fit in with it!

3. ACCESS TO THE INTERNET

The Internet is one of the most essential tools for spreading Fake News. It's like it was especially designed to help get the Fake News message out there. It enables you to bypass the Mainstream Media and communicate directly with those interested in what you have to say. And by that, I mean the deluded and ill-informed.

 Donald Trump   ● Follow

Thanks to the Internet people don't have to rely on the mainstream media's Fake News. I can get my Fake News directly to them instead.

4. ENEMIES

Enemies are another vital factor that you will need to promulgate Fake News. You can then blame anything bad that happens to you or anyone else on your enemies – it doesn't matter if they're guilty or not! And if you don't have any enemies, just choose someone at random and blame them. And then they will soon become your enemy even if they weren't before!

//

THINGS PEOPLE MAY SAY IMMEDIATELY AFTER YOU'VE TOLD THEM A BIT OF FAKE NEWS

- Eh?

- You what?

- Did I hear that right?

- No, I don't think so

- Well, that's an interesting opinion

- Are you quite sure about that?

- Sorry – I may have misunderstood. Could you repeat that slowly?

- You are joking, right?

- Ha ha ha ha... Oh my God! You were serious just then, weren't you?

- Could you talk me through that again and show your working at the same time?

- Is it just me or was that just complete bollocks?

- You're talking out of your arse, mate!

- Are you flipping well insane?

- Sound the alarm! Total bollocks alert!

///

TIMES YOU MAY WANT TO USE FAKE NEWS WHEN YOU'RE AT WORK

- When you have to come up with excuses for being late

- When you have to come up with excuses for not having done the stuff you were asked to

- When you need to explain the list of expenses you want to claim for following a recent business trip

- When you have to get up to make a presentation for which you have done no preparation whatsoever

- When a significant proportion of the contents of the stationery cupboard are found hidden about your person as you are leaving the office

- When you have to explain a sudden downturn in profits in an area for which you are responsible

- When it becomes known that a large amount of company funds has been mysteriously diverted into your personal bank account

- When you need to heap blame on someone else for a monumental cock up for which you were entirely responsible

- When you need to come up with an excuse for being found rummaging around in your boss's office and/or using his desk as a toilet

PHRASES YOU SHOULD AVOID USING WHILE GIVING OUT FAKE NEWS

- Did I really say that out loud?

- Wow! I can't believe you fell for that one!

- You should see the looks on your faces as I'm telling you these things!

- Even though you know I am a pathological liar – please trust me on this one

- Before I start, I should let you all know that I have been officially certified as a pathological liar

- Every single thing I have just told you today is untrue with one exception. That was it just then

- The following statement is a massive lie and you're all stupid if you believe it

- Did you hear what I just said? What the hell have I been smoking?

- To be honest I don't really know what I'm talking about

BODY LANGUAGE YOU SHOULD AVOID WHEN ANNOUNCING LIES AND FAKE NEWS

1. SHAKING YOUR HEAD

If you are announcing a massive lie to anyone, do not fall into the trap of shaking your head from side to side while you are speaking. This gesture may communicate a silent message to everyone watching. It will be as though you are signalling to everyone, "No! No! No! No way! Oh my God! No!" If your head does start shaking like this while you are speaking, it may be the effect of your soul becoming possessed by guilt at the insidious and deceitful things you are saying and desperately trying to send a signal up through your neck to warn the world.

Avoid this at all costs if you want to be a successful proponent of Fake News!

2. CLENCHED BUTTOCKS

Your buttocks gradually clenching together is another sign of tension that may result from acting in a dishonest manner while intentionally deceiving others. Again, you should avoid letting anyone see that your body has reacted in this manner. If you have just announced a major new piece of Fake News to a large group of people and feel your buttocks clenching in anxiety behind you, try and avoid the temptation to slowly turn your back to them and drop your trousers in order to reveal your clenched buttocks. You should however employ a professional buttock masseur to unclench your cheeks. If the problem is not addressed, the clenching may spread all around your body until you are literally consumed by your own tense buttocks and disappear up your own backside.

 Donald Trump

I like to keep fit by clenching my buttocks several times a day. And whenever I meet anyone I'm pretty sure they're clenching theirs too.

3. LOOK OF HORROR OR DISGUST

Similar to above. A look of horror may creep onto your face as another unconscious reaction when you are enunciating a juicy piece of Fake News. It is unfortunately a natural response for the body and face to react in an appalled manner when the stench of lies and falsehood is detected. For this reason your face may unconsciously form itself into a look that will tell anyone watching, "The stuff I'm telling you now is an absolute steaming pile of lies. I am disgusted with myself."

4. SWEATING AND TREMBLING

Another effect that excessive lying may have on your body is that you start to become stressed and begin sweating, trembling and hyperventilating. This may become noticeable to people if sweat starts pouring off you to such an extent that it short circuits nearby electrical equipment and you single-handedly manage to raise the temperature of the room forcing someone to open a window and let some air in. Whose side is your body on? It's doing you no favours here. If this sort of thing happens every time you say something untrue, it may be best to tell everyone you are announcing your piece of Fake News using a form of interpretative dance.

5. WINKING

This really is a giveaway. Under no circumstances should you conclude a piece of Fake News with a sly wink. This is like a visual punctuation mark to denote that the previous statement you made was a naughty lie. Winking in these circumstances is done by very dim people labouring under the misapprehension that others enjoy being blatantly lied to and regard attempts to con them as a bit of cheeky fun.

6. RAISED EYEBROWS

This is even worse than the sly wink. It will be even worse again if you employ the Roger Moore special by raising just one of your eyebrows. Hence the expression "Less is Moore". Similarly try to avoid stroking your chin or miming your nose extending from your face like Pinocchio's.

FAKE SPORTS

"HALF THE LIES THEY TELL ABOUT ME AREN'T TRUE."

— Yogi Berra

THAT'S NOT VERY SPORTING – FAKE NEWS IN THE WORLD OF SPORT

SPORT IS A WONDERFUL THING. It enables people from all levels of society to get out in the fresh air and partake in something exciting, invigorating and requiring considerable skill. Yes, we're talking about cheating.

Sport is perfectly designed not only for the pursuit of excellence but also for the pursuit of Fake News. It's a great way to make people think you are a little more excellent than is really the case!

TOUR DE FARCE

Lance Armstrong won the 1993 UCI Road World Championships, overcame cancer that medical experts thought would be fatal and won the Tour de France every year between 1999 to 2005.

A federal enquiry into allegations of doping was held between 2010

LOCHTE IN THE TOILET

and 2012 but made no charges. An investigation by the United States Anti-Doping Agency, however, led to a lifetime ban from all sports and the stripping of all his achievements back to his first Tour de France win.

In January 2013 Armstrong was interviewed on TV by Oprah Winfrey and confessed to the use of performance enhancing drugs over a significant proportion of his career.

Since his lifetime ban, Armstrong has lost all his major sponsorships and been forced to pay back over $10 million in damages and legal settlements. So, perhaps the doping wasn't really worth it after all!

Even worse – recent research has suggested that EPO, the drug he predominantly used, may not have provided any advantages at all. Armstrong may have been cheating for all those years using a substance which didn't actually help him! The drug itself may have been Fake News!

Does this mean that Armstrong can now sue the manufacturers of EPO for all the losses he suffered as a result of cheating using their performance-not-so-enhancing drug?

Ryan Lochte is an extraordinarily successful professional swimmer but, after winning 12 Olympic medals, he then slightly sullied his reputation during the Rio Olympics.

In August 2016, Lochte claimed that he and fellow swimmer Jimmy Feigen along with two other teammates had been held up, forced out of their taxi and robbed at gunpoint in Rio de Janeiro.

The Brazilian Olympic organizers were mortified at the news. CCTV footage from the scene of the crime however revealed a slightly different story.

The swimmers had not been held up but had instead vandalized a toilet at a petrol station while intoxicated. Lochte was banned from the sport for 10 months, and possibly banned from the petrol station's toilets for even longer.

A HOLE IN KIM JONG

The greatest golfer to have ever lived is, of course, our old friend former North Korean leader Kim Jong Il. He not only achieved more than any other golfer in history but he managed to do it all in a career which only lasted one afternoon.

According to North Korean media, in October 1994, Kim Jong Il achieved a record breaking round of golf. He scored 11 holes in one and achieved a score of 38 under par.

And if that wasn't good enough, it was his first ever try at playing golf. Despite clearly being a born natural, Kim Jong decided to retire from the sport immediately. It's always best to quit while you're ahead, isn't it?

In case you are thinking his achievement sounds unlikely, there were 17 witnesses to the event. OK, they were all employed by Kim Jong Il as his bodyguards. But they definitely saw it happen!

FAKE PARALYMPIANS!

At the Paralympics in Sydney in 2000, Spain's team won gold in the intellectual disability basketball contest.

There was just one problem. One of the victorious Spanish basketball players let slip that ten out of the 12 members of the team were not disabled.

Spain were stripped of their win and the team had to return their gold medals.

THE JOY OF SOX

How do you get a team of great sportsmen to lose the World Series and ruin their careers? Simple – don't pay them enough!

The Black Sox Scandal was a conspiracy to fix the Baseball World Series played in 1919 between the Cincinnati Reds and Chicago White Sox.

The White Sox were by far the favourites to win. They were perhaps the greatest side ever to play the game. Unfortunately, while they may have been great players, they were not being paid very much money. As a result, some of the team were open to alternative sources of income.

The team, however, was split. A group of more straitlaced players would never countenance dishonest behaviour. Supposedly these players never spoke to their less ethically minded colleagues on or off the field.

After the Cincinnati Reds unexpectedly won the series, eight members of the White Sox, including their star hitter "Shoeless" Joe Jackson, were put on trial and ultimately banned for life from the sport. Following the trial some members of the team tried

to organize a tour but this had to be abandoned when it was made known that anyone who played them would also receive a lifetime ban.

They then tried to play exhibition games in Chicago each Sunday until the city council threatened to take away the license of any ballpark that allowed them to appear. The White Sox would not win another American League championship until 1959.

IT'S NOT CRICKET

Cricket is, of course, the great game of fair-minded, sporting English gentlemen. And as such, it has been subject to match-fixing for two hundred years.

William Lambert played cricket for Surrey and the MCC in the early 19th century. In July 1817 in a match between Surrey and Epsom (or perhaps more accurately between Epsom and Surrey-Not-Including-Epsom), Lambert became the first player in history to score a century in both innings of a first-class match.

Sadly, this turned out to be Lambert's final first-class appearance. His career was then ended as a result of an earlier game in which both sides had been attempting to lose. To some observers, it must seem as though games like that are quite common in cricket.

The offending match had been played between Nottingham and England (or perhaps more accurately between Nottingham and England-Not-Including-Nottingham).

In the end, England turned out to be better at losing than Nottingham. In fact, the England team have since become so good at losing they can now do it without even having to try!

Lord Frederick Beauclerk, a long-time rival of Lambert's, took exception to Lambert's performance and the fact he had been seen leaving the ground with a large brown envelope, presumed to be full of bank-notes.

Beauclerk took his complaint to the MCC who banned Lambert for life – not for accepting money but for not having tried hard enough. In fact, Lambert was merely the fall guy in an attempt to stop the rigging of matches.

After all, Lambert's side had in fact won the game! Maybe he should have been found guilty of not trying hard enough to lose!

BAD
PRESIDENTS

**"I WAS NOT LYING, I SAID THINGS THAT
LATER ON SEEMED TO BE UNTRUE."**

— Richard Nixon

DODGY BEHAVIOUR AND CLASSIC FAKE NEWS
BY FORMER US PRESIDENTS

THE USA'S FIRST PRESIDENT **GEORGE WASHINGTON** famously told his father, "I cannot tell a lie!" As a result of his inability to dissemble, young George admitted he was responsible for the sad fate of his father's favourite cherry tree: "I did cut it with my hatchet."

In fact, the entire story is untrue. The event probably never happened and appeared for the first time in the fifth edition of Washington's biography published in 1806 some years after his death.

It was therefore, once again, all Fake News!

But this was Fake News that carried an important lesson – you should never lie!

Or more to the point – you should never get caught telling a lie!

And the other even more important lesson for Fake News enthusiasts is that people will always remember a bit of Fake News as long as it sounds like a decent story.

In 1800, the USA held what was only the fourth presidential election in the country's history. Even at this stage the campaign was dominated by negative campaigning, slanderous accusations and Fake News.

This was all highly unfortunate as the two candidates were the previous president John Adams and the previous vice-president Thomas Jefferson.

Adams' supporters issued warnings that if Jefferson won, "We would see our wives and daughters the victims of legal prostitution," and, "murder, robbery, rape, adultery and incest will openly be taught and practiced."

Jefferson was also accused of having fathered a number of children by the slaves he owned and of robbing a widow and her children of their trust fund. And, in a particularly desperate move, Adams' side claimed that Jefferson was in fact dead!

The 1828 election between John Quincy Adams and Andrew Jackson was characterized by more ill-tempered mudslinging and questionable accusations.

Jackson's wife was accused of bigamy – which was technically true.

In response, Adams was accused of having procured an American girl to satisfy the Russian Czar during the time when he was Minister to Russia.

Adams' supporters meanwhile accused Jackson of being a gambling, murdering, slave trader. Jackson won the election but a few weeks later his wife died from a heart attack.

Jackson duly accused Adams and his supporters of having murdered her.

In 1840, presidential candidate William Henry Harrison presented himself as the log cabin candidate. In other words, he was a simple man of the people.

Well, he certainly owned a log cabin, but he had been born to wealthy and influential plantation owners in Virginia.

Even Abraham Lincoln practiced a degree of political deceit and

pretended not to be too far ahead of opinion by telling the public and political allies that he didn't believe in political equality for slaves.

In 1987, following the Iran-Contra affair, Ronald Reagan went on television to say, "A few months ago I told the American people I did not trade arms for hostages. My heart and my best intentions still tell me that's true, but the facts and the evidence tell me it is not."

So, that is a great way to avoid admitting you were lying while acknowledging the existence of clear evidence that you've been caught lying!

On another occasion Reagan said, "I'm not smart enough to lie."

Or could that have been a cunning double bluff made by someone who was just about smart enough to lie?

BAD PRESIDENTS

In 1998, President Bill Clinton said of Monica Lewinsky, "I did not have sexual relations with that woman." Unfortunately, Lewinsky had not yet got around to emptying her laundry basket. Evidence duly emerged that Clinton had at least had sexual relations with her dress.

But, of course, the most famous example of US Presidential dissembling must be Watergate.

In November 1972, Republican party candidate Richard Nixon was re-elected as President of the USA with 60.67 per cent of the popular vote.

No president since has polled better. What could possibly go wrong?

The answer is nothing – it had already gone wrong!

On Saturday June 17, 1972, in the run up to Nixon's re-election, five men had been arrested after breaking into the rival Democratic Party's headquarters in the Watergate complex in Washington DC.

It emerged that a previous break-in had been carried out to bug phones at the Democrats' HQ.

This second break-in turned out to have been a maintenance exercise because the bugs that had originally been planted weren't working properly!

A money trail emerged showing that the burglars had connections stretching back to Nixon's re-election campaign.

Nixon insisted he had nothing to do with the break-in and knew nothing about it. Luckily, it turned out that Nixon taped everything that occurred in the Oval Office.

The tapes were subpoenaed by special prosecutor Archibald Cox, appointed to investigate Watergate.

Nixon refused to release the tapes and then attempted to get Cox fired.

Not only did this make Nixon look ever-so-slightly guilty, the Attorney General and Deputy Attorney General both resigned rather than fire the special prosecutor.

Nixon then asked his Solicitor General to fire Cox. This time the Solicitor General only considered resigning but then went ahead with the firing anyway.

A new special prosecutor was appointed and Nixon was ultimately forced to release his tapes after all. But wouldn't you know it – a possibly crucial part of the tapes recorded on June 20, 1972 just after the break in, had been accidentally erased!

The tapes did however reveal several things.

Firstly, Nixon swore like a trooper – it was as a result of publication of the tape transcripts that the phrase "expletive deleted" entered popular parlance.

Also, Nixon was on tape discussing paying hush money to the burglars.

And, finally, Nixon was on tape on June 23, 1972, discussing how to stop the FBI investigation into the break-in.

In November 1973, Nixon had declared in a TV question and answer session, "People have got to know whether or not their President is a crook. Well, I'm not a crook. I've earned everything I've got."

It was, of course, all Fake News – Nixon was a crook after all.

Was Nixon responsible for the break-in? This is possibly Fake News as well.

The tapes revealed Nixon asking, "Who was the a**hole who ordered it?"

In the end, it was not the conspiracy itself but the cover-up that brought Nixon down and forced him to resign as US President on August 8, 1974.

Since Watergate all political scandals have been denoted by the suffix -gate.

So, perhaps Watergate should be known as Watergate-gate.